THE WEAVING WORKS
4717 Brooklyn Ave NE Seattle WA 98105
Ph: 206-524-1221 Fax: 206-524-0250

ori ami knits

FIBER GEOMETRY

OLGA BURAYA-KEFELIAN   AND   VANESSA YAP-EINBUND

From Olga
To my husband, Jason, my parents and my friends, whose constant love,
support and belief in me have enabled me to do what I love.

From Vanessa
To my husband, Paul, family and friends, thank you for your immense
support, without you this book would not have been possible.

Published in 2010 by Olga Buraya-Kefelian and Vanessa Yap-Einbund via Craft Press.

Text copyright © 2010 Ori Ami Knits: Fiber Geometry. Olga Buraya-Kefelian and Vanessa Yap-Einbund
Photographs copyright © 2010 Vanessa Yap-Einbund

Buraya-Kefelian, Olga, Yap-Einbund, Vanessa
Ori Ami Knits: Fiber Geometry
ISBN-13: 978-0-96-55451-8-1

Every effort has been made to ensure that all the information in this book is accurate. However, due to
different conditions, tools, and individual skills, the publishers cannot be responsible for any injuries,
losses, and other damages that may result from the use of the information in this book.

Editors: Olga Buraya-Kefelian, Vanessa Yap-Einbund, and Yahaira Ferreira
Layout designer, Illustrator, Photographer: Vanessa Yap-Einbund
Technical Editors: Alexandra Virgiel and Jenn Jarvis
Styling: Olga Buraya-Kefelian, Vanessa Yap-Einbund, Kirsten Johnstone
Website design and programming: Vanessa Yap-Einbund, Priscilla Meredith, Mac Liaw

Printed by Craft Press, Inc. 111 Quint Street, San Francisco, CA 94124 (415) 826-3000

Manufactured in China.

Distributed directly by Ori Ami Knits.
www.oriamiknits.com
For wholesale information, questions or comments, please contact info@oriamiknits.com

CONTENTS

INTRODUCTION

Ori (jap.) fold, weave
Amimono (jap.) knit, knitting

Folding. Pleating. Draping. Combining textures. These are the concepts driving this collection.

Creating clothing using fiber blends such as bamboo, soy, corn, milk protein, steel, silk and seaweed has transformed the way we craft. In the pursuit of minimalism and adaptability, we show some of the best ways these fibers can be sculpted into exquisite garments, whether in surprising combinations or alone.

The 13 pieces in this collection, all featuring Habu Textiles, create a wardrobe that expresses personal style and aesthetic. In each garment design, we seek versatility to provide clothing that intermixes with and complements one's existing wardrobe, or perhaps provides a feature piece to complete an outfit. Each yarn combination for the collection was selected with purpose, with yarn and design only coming together after considering the fiber's weight, texture and color. Our preference for solid color balances the intricate and architectural details shown throughout this collection.

Ori Ami Knits is divided into four concepts. In "Practical Geometry", simple shapes are enhanced by innovative construction and stitch detailing. The construction of the Rhombus wrap provides the wearer with multiple styles built into one garment; the complex stitch of the Axonometric top emphasizes the depth in a shape of a diamond. Effortless, minimalist garments that work as every day or evening pieces fill "Subtle Layers". The Duplicity pullover is a playful take on the layering trend. The smart construction of the Arcus pullover creates a sophisticated sweater with multiple folds gathered around the shoulders. In "Dimensional Folds" we experiment with texture and folds to achieve one-of-a-kind details such as the neckline found in the Concertina dress and the versatile fit of the Airfoil skirt. "Nautical Structures" explores the detailing found in underwater structures, be it the rich colors in the Corallium scarf or the great feathery seaweed textures of the Japonica cravat.

To insure that our designs were in line with our original vision, we did not stop with design. We took on the entire publishing process from the publication concept, garment styling, photography to layout. We hope you enjoy our work and find favorites for years to come!

DESIGNERS

Olga Buraya-Kefelian has been knitting for many years. Her mother taught her to knit at a very young age, and Olga started designing in her late teens. Although a linguist by education, in 2006 she made her first attempt to design for a publication. Her contributing designs have graced the book covers of Sensual Knits and Pure Knits. Coming from a family of a professional tailor, Olga acquired her cloth-ing construction knowledge early, which has become more intuitive through the years. This intuition helps her to create imaginative yet versatile knitwear. While working on her own style and designs, she has designed for multiple magazines such as Knitty, Interweave Knits and Crochet. Olga has also designed patterns for Blue Sky Alpacas, Spud and Chloe and ShibuiKnits.

Currently, Olga lives in Japan and is working on self-publishing a line of knitwear patterns, but she enjoys the challenge of joining minds with other creative souls to craft one cohesive body of work. She believes that each garment has its own story and purpose within the world of fashion. She fulfills her vision by gathering inspiration from industrial and architectural designs and combining them with her own interpretations of European and Japanese designs. While she uses knitwear design as her canvas, her designs are heavily influenced by the fiber – the very essence of the material. In Ori Ami Knits, her exploration of Habu Textiles' uniqueness demonstrates her thoughtful expression of modern design concepts.

Vanessa Yap-Einbund is a San Francisco-based graphic designer, freelance photographer and an avid knitter. Her minimalistic approach to photography and design often reflects a sense of clarity and peace to viewers. Being the first grand daughter that was born in her family, Vanessa's grandfather gave her a name in kanji · "文静" meaning gentle and quiet which is an immediate translation of her personal aesthetic. Vanessa's designs are sparse with minimal details · they do not stop on paper. Meticulously thought out, her designs incorporate what she sees in nature.

Vanessa's inspiration derives from everyday objects and nature. Her love for nature never stops, even her tiny apartment work area is surrounded with moss, lichens, twigs and of course all sorts of Habu cones/yarn she has collected over the years. Vanessa has a deep appreciation of natural fibers. She en-joys exploring the tones, textures, nuances and range of sepias inherent in every natural fiber especially those supplied by Habu Textiles. The interplay of simple basic stitches and natural colors excites her more than anything else. Vanessa tends to choose fibers such as wool or silk, though her love for silk stainless steel has grown increasingly since discovering Habu Textiles about six years ago. Her current favorites include cotton gima, tokken viscose silk, handspun tassar silk, linen paper and tsumugi combi-nation all from Habu Textiles.

Kirsten Johnstone is an architect and designer based in Melbourne, Australia with a passion for efficient modern design. She explores this interest through a variety of mediums: built, knit, sewn, photographed and written. Kirsten's minimalist and clean aesthetic results in a deceptively simple, fresh and elegant response.

Kirsten's designs seek to eliminate unnecessary detail and provide a pure and lean line and form. These designs work effectively with the incredibly diverse range of textural modern yarns sourced and supplied by Habu Textiles. Kirsten will often make a number of swatches from a particular yarn and then closely observe its response to different environments and conditions over time for her design to emerge. You will often find swatches in her pockets and see her fondling them while waiting for her children to finish school! Kirsten has a particular interest in the more 'structural' yarns available from Habu, including silk stainless steel, kibiso silk and naturally raw yarns such as linen and recycled netting.

chapter one

PRACTICAL GEOMETRY

CUBED NECKLACE
立方体の首飾り

An eclectic piece of jewelry can always dress up the simplest outfit. Knit from a vibrant color of silk in the shape of a cube, this necklace acquires a character of its own. Express yourself with this handmade piece of jewelry that can be created just in time for the party.

by OLGA BURAYA·KEFELIAN

SIZE
Length 24in/61cm
Cube measured at edge 1in/2.5cm

YARN
Habu Textiles N-6B root (konyaku) sizing silk, 100% silk;
177yds(160m)/oz(28g); 5 (red) Main yarn
1oz/28g OR 177yds/160m
Worked with 2 strands held together

Habu Textiles A-189 cotton jersey tape, 100% cotton;
44yds(42)/oz(28g); 250 (black) Cord yarn
1oz/28g OR 44yds(42m)

NEEDLES
2.25 mm dpns, set of 5 (or size to obtain gauge)

NOTIONS
Stitch markers
Scrap yarn of similar weight as Main Yarn
Crochet hook
Sewing needle
Matching thread
Plastic pellets or bamboo fill (not polyfill)

GAUGE
36 sts and 52 rows in 4in/10cm over washed and blocked St st
swatch with 2 strands of Main Yarn held together

INSTRUCTIONS
Cube (make 4, or as desired)
Using Provisional method with scrap yarn and crochet hook CO
7 sts onto 1 dpn.
Switch to Main Yarn.

Row 1 (RS): K.
Row 2 (WS): K. (ridge)
Beginning with a K row, work 11 rows in St st.

Next row (WS): K. (ridge) Do not turn work at end of this row.
With WS facing, using a second dpn pick up and knit 9 sts along
the left edge of the square.
Remove scrap yarn from the CO and put those 7 sts on a third
dpn, then purl across those sts.
With a fourth dpn pick up 9 sts along the right edge of the
square and pm at the end to indicate the beg of the round.

Round 1
Ndl 1: P across 7 sts.
Ndl 2: K1, p7, k1.
Ndl 3: P across 7 sts.
Ndl 4: K1, p7, k1.

Round 2
Ndl 1: P across 7 sts.
Ndl 2: Sl1wyif, p7, sl1wyif.
Ndl 3: P across 7 sts.
Ndl 4: Sl1wyif, p7, sl1wyif.

Repeat Rnds 1-2 four times more, then Rnd 1 only once (total of
11 rnds worked).

Next round (decrease and ridge)
Ndl 1: K7.
Ndl 2: K2tog, k5, ssk.
Ndl 3: K7.
Ndl 4: K2tog, k5, ssk.

Now ONLY work on Ndl 1. (Leave other sts on their needles.)
Beg with a K row, work 9 rows St st.
Stuff your cube with plastic pellets or bamboo fill.
Graft (Kitchener stitch) the sts of Ndl 1 and Ndl 3 together.
Kitchener stitch the sts of Ndl 2 and Ndl 4 to the corresponding
sides of the square, using a single strand of Main Yarn.

FINISHING

Cut three 36in/91.5cm strands of Cord Yarns. Measure along your neckline to decide on the length of your necklace and trim accordingly. Tie the three strands together with a knot at each end, leaving 2-3in/5-7.5cm ends. Place the cubes evenly along the cord, pin in place and sew them to the three strands using sewing needle and matching thread.

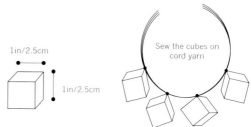

1in/2.5cm

1in/2.5cm

Sew the cubes on cord yarn

RHOMBUS WRAP
菱形のラップ

A modern transformable wrap made from an unusually
dyed fiber. This fiber has a unique twist that contributes
not only to the texture but to the depth of the finished
garment. Knit in one piece from side to side, this
project will be a breeze to make. Simple armhole slits
and subtle angled front edges provide elegant detailing.
This wrap can be worn in a variety of styles. Experiment
to find the way you like it best!

by KIRSTEN JOHNSTONE

To fit bust size [32, 34, 36][38, 40, 42, 44] [46, 48, 50]in/
[81, 86.5, 91.5][96.5, 101.5, 106.5, 112][117, 122, 127]cm

Length (worn long way)
[24, 24.5, 25][25.75, 26.25, 26.75, 27.25][28, 28.5, 29]in/
[61, 62, 63.5][65.25, 66.5, 67.75, 69][71, 72.25, 73.5]cm

YARN
Habu Textiles A-134 10/2x5 Aresco, 100% Cotton;
158yds(142m)/oz(28g); 12 (yellow)
[11, 11, 12][13, 13, 14, 15][15, 16, 17]oz/[308, 308, 341]
[364, 364, 392, 420][420, 448, 476]g
OR
[1632, 1734, 1836][1938, 2040, 2142, 2244][2346, 2448,
2550]yds/[1538, 1634, 1730][1827, 1923, 2019, 2115][2211,
2307, 2403]m
Worked with 2 strands held together

NEEDLES
4.5 mm circular (or size to obtain gauge)

NOTIONS
Tapestry needle
1 or 2 shawl/kilt pins
Crochet hook (Optional)

GAUGE
22 sts and 32 rows in 4in/10cm in Float st pattern with 2
strands held together

FLOAT STITCH PATTERN
Row 1 (RS): P3, *k2, sl1wyib kwise*, repeat from * till 3 sts rem, p3.
Row 2 (WS): K3, *sl the sl st wyif pwise, p2*, repeat from * till 3
sts rem, k3.
Row 3: P3, *k2, k into back of sl st*, repeat from * till 3 sts rem, p3.
Row 4: K3, p till 3 sts rem, k3.
Row 5: P3, k1, *sl1wyib kwise, k2*, repeat from * till 5 sts rem,
sl1wyib kwise, k1, p3.
Row 6: K3, p1, *sl the sl st wyif pwise, p2*, repeat from * till 5 sts
rem, sl1wyif pwise, p1, k3.
Row 7: P3, k1, *k into back of sl st, k2*, repeat from * till 5 sts
rem, k into back of sl st, k1, p3.
Row 8: K3, p till 3 sts rem, k3.
Row 9: P3, *sl1wyif kwise, k2*, repeat from * till 3 sts rem, p3.
Row 10: K3, *p2, sl the slipped st wyib pwise*, repeat from * till
3 sts rem, k3.
Row 11: P3, *k into back of sl st, k2*, repeat from * till 3 sts
rem, p3.
Row 12: K3, p till 3 sts rem, k3.
Repeat Rows 1-12.

BODY
Right front
With 2 strands of yarn held together, CO [132, 135, 138]
[141, 144, 147, 150][153, 156, 159] sts.
Row 1 (RS): P3, k to last 3 sts, p3.
Row 2 (WS): K3, p to last 3 sts, k3.

Start working Float st pattern (see above).
AT THE SAME TIME

Right front short row shaping
Note: As you work the short rows on this side, pick up and k the
wraps together with the sts they are wrapped around on the next
RS row.
Row 3 (RS): Work [8, 10, 11][12, 14, 6, 8][9, 11, 12] sts, sl next
st, w&t.
Row 4 (WS): Work back in patt.
Row 5 and all RS rows: Work to [6, 6, 6][6, 6, 7, 7][7, 7, 7] sts
past the previous wrapped st, sl next st, w&t.
Row 6 and all WS rows: Work back in patt.
Repeat Rows 5-6 until you have made a total of 19 wraps (38
short rows).
Row 41: Work to last [8, 9, 11][13, 14, 6, 7][9, 10, 12] sts, sl
next st, w&t.
Row 42: Work back in patt.

Work even over all sts in Float st patt for [54, 58, 62][66, 70,
74, 78][82, 86, 90] rows.

Shape right armhole
(RS): Work [34, 34, 34][34, 34, 36, 36][36, 36, 36], BO [37, 38, 40][41, 42, 44, 45][47, 48, 49], work [61, 63, 64][66, 68, 67, 69][70, 72, 74] sts.
(WS): Work [61, 63, 64][66, 68, 67, 69][70, 72, 74], Backward loop CO [37, 38, 40][41, 42, 44, 45][47, 48, 49], work [34, 34, 34][34, 34, 36, 36][36, 36, 36] sts to end.

Back
Work even in Float st patt for [102, 110, 118][126, 134, 142, 150][158, 166, 174] rows.

Shape left armhole
(RS): Work [34, 34, 34][34, 34, 36, 36][36, 36, 36], BO [37, 38, 40][41, 42, 44, 45][47, 48, 49], work [61, 63, 64][66, 68, 67, 69][70, 72, 74] sts.
(WS): Work [61, 63, 64][66, 68, 67, 69][70, 72, 74], Backward loop CO [37, 38, 40][41, 42, 44, 45][47, 48, 49], work [34, 34, 34][34, 34, 36, 36][36, 36, 36] sts to end.

Left front
Continue working straight in Float st patt for another [88, 92, 96][100, 104, 108, 112][116, 120, 122] rows.

Left front short row shaping

Row 1 (RS): Work to last [8, 9, 11][13, 14, 6, 7][9, 10, 12] sts, sl next st, w&t.

Row 2 (WS): Work back in patt.

Row 3 and all RS rows: Work to [6, 6, 6][6, 6, 7, 7][7, 7, 7] sts before the previous wrapped st, sl next st, w&t.

Row 4 and all WS rows: Work back in patt.

Repeat Rows 3-4 until you have made a total of 19 wraps (38 short rows).

Row 39: Work [8, 10, 11][12, 14, 6, 8][9, 11, 12] sts, sl next st, w&t.

Row 40: Work back in patt.

Row 41 (RS): P3, k picking up all the wraps and working them together with the sts they are wrapped around till 3 sts rem, p3.

Row 42 (WS): BO 3 sts in k, BO in p to last 3 sts, BO rem sts in k.

FINISHING

Cut yarn. Weave in ends. Gently soak and block the wrap.

Tip: To stop edges from curling you may want to work a round of single crochet around the armholes.

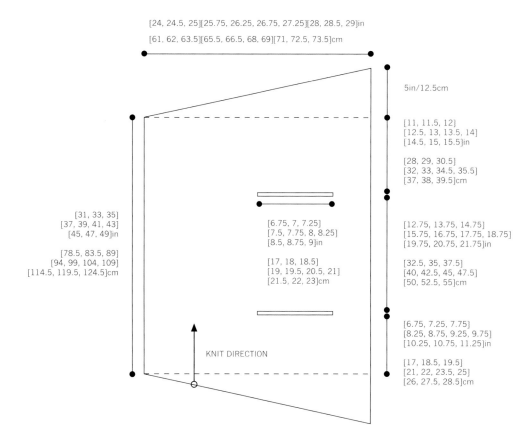

[24, 24.5, 25][25.75, 26.25, 26.75, 27.25][28, 28.5, 29]in
[61, 62, 63.5][65.5, 66.5, 68, 69][71, 72.5, 73.5]cm

5in/12.5cm

[11, 11.5, 12]
[12.5, 13, 13.5, 14]
[14.5, 15, 15.5]in

[28, 29, 30.5]
[32, 33, 34.5, 35.5]
[37, 38, 39.5]cm

[31, 33, 35]
[37, 39, 41, 43]
[45, 47, 49]in

[78.5, 83.5, 89]
[94, 99, 104, 109]
[114.5, 119.5, 124.5]cm

[6.75, 7, 7.25]
[7.5, 7.75, 8, 8.25]
[8.5, 8.75, 9]in

[17, 18, 18.5]
[19, 19.5, 20.5, 21]
[21.5, 22, 23]cm

[12.75, 13.75, 14.75]
[15.75, 16.75, 17.75, 18.75]
[19.75, 20.75, 21.75]in

[32.5, 35, 37.5]
[40, 42.5, 45, 47.5]
[50, 52.5, 55]cm

[6.75, 7.25, 7.75]
[8.25, 8.75, 9.25, 9.75]
[10.25, 10.75, 11.25]in

[17, 18.5, 19.5]
[21, 22, 23.5, 25]
[26, 27.5, 28.5]cm

KNIT DIRECTION

AXONOMETRIC TOP
不等角投影の上着

This original axonometric diamond stitch design is
perfectly expressed with this crisp yarn. The essential
beauty of the pattern is revealed through movement and
the inherent quality of the fiber, which allows the pleats
to acquire greater depth than visible to the naked eye.

by OLGA BURAYA·KEFELIAN

SIZES

To fit bust size [32, 34, 36][38, 40, 42, 44][46, 48, 50]in/[81, 86.5, 91.5][96.5, 101.5, 106.5, 112][117, 122, 127]cm

Finished measurements [35.25, 37.25, 39][41, 42.75, 44.5, 46.5][48.25, 50, 52]in/[89.5, 94.5, 99][104, 108.5, 113, 118][122.5, 127, 132]cm

Length [21.5, 21.75, 22][22.25, 22.75, 23, 23.75][24, 24.25, 25]in/[54.5, 55, 56][56.5, 58, 58.5, 60.5][61, 61.5, 63.5]cm

YARN

Habu Textiles A-174 cotton gima, 100% cotton; 265 yds (238m)/oz(28 g); 7 (mustard)
[7, 8, 8][9, 9, 10, 10][11, 11, 12]oz/[200, 212, 224][237, 249, 262, 274][287, 299, 312]g
OR
[1885, 2003, 2120][2283, 2356, 2474, 2592][2709, 2827, 2945]yds/[1693, 1799, 1904][2010, 2116, 2222, 2328][2433, 2539, 2645]m
Worked with 2 strands held together

NEEDLES

3.5 mm and 2.75 mm (or size to obtain gauge)

NOTIONS

Cable needle
Crochet hook
Scrap yarn in same weight
Stitch holders
Stitch markers
Tapestry needle
Spare needle

GAUGE

26 sts and 40 rows in 4in/10cm over washed and blocked
Diamond st patt on bigger needle with 2 strands held together

DIAMOND STITCH PATTERN (18 sts repeat)

R1 (RS): *K6, ssk, m1r, sl wyif, m1l, k2tog, k6, sl wyif*.
R2 (WS): *P7, sl wyif, p3, sl wyif, p6*.
R3: *K5, ssk, m1r, k1, sl wyif, k1, m1l, k2tog, k5, sl wyif*.
R4: *P6, sl wyif, p5, sl wyif, p5*.
R5: *K4, ssk, m1r, k2, sl wyif, k2, m1l, k2tog, k4, sl wyif*.
R6: *P5, sl wyif, p7, sl wyif, p4*.
R7: *K3, ssk, m1r, k3, sl wyif, k3, m1l, k2tog, k3, sl wyif*.
R8: *P4, sl wyif, p9, sl wyif, p3*.
R9: *K2, ssk, m1r, k4, sl wyif, k4, m1l, k2tog, k2, sl wyif*.
R10: *P3, sl wyif, p11, sl wyif, p2*.
R11: *K1, ssk, m1r, k5, sl wyif, k5, m1l, k2tog, k1, sl wyif*.
R12: *P2, sl wyif, p13, sl wyif, p1*.
R13: *Ssk, m1r, k6, sl wyif, k6, m1l, k2tog, sl wyif*.
R14: *P1, sl wyif, p15, sl wyif*.
R15: *K7, sl wyif, k7, 1/1 left cross PB*.
R16: *P18*.
R17: *M1l, k2tog, k6, sl wyif, k6, ssk, m1r, sl wyif*.
R18: *P2, sl wyif, p13, sl wyif, p1*.
R19: *K1, m1l, k2tog, k5, sl wyif, k5, ssk, m1r, k1, sl wyif*.
R20: *P3, sl wyif, p11, sl wyif, p2*.
R21: *K2, m1l, k2tog, k4, sl wyif, k4, ssk, m1r, k2, sl wyif*.
R22: *P4, sl wyif, p9, sl wyif, p3*.
R23: *K3, m1l, k2tog, k3, sl wyif, k3, ssk, m1r, k3, sl wyif*.
R24: *P5, sl wyif, p7, sl wyif, p4*.
R25: *K4, m1l, k2tog, k2, sl wyif, k2, ssk, m1r, k4, sl wyif*.
R26: *P6, sl wyif, p5, sl wyif, p5*.
R27: *K5, m1l, k2tog, k1, sl wyif, k1, ssk, m1r, k5, sl wyif*.
R28: *P7, sl wyif, p3, sl wyif, p6*.
R29: *P6, m1l, k2tog, sl wyif, ssk, m1r, k6, sl wyif*.
R30: *P8, sl wyif, p1, sl wyif, p7*.
R31: *K7, 1/1 right cross PB, k7, sl wyif*.
R32: *P18*.

FRONT

Hem

Using Provisional method with crochet hook and scrap yarn CO [115, 121, 127][133, 139, 145, 151][157, 163, 169] sts on larger needle.
Switch to Main yarn.
Work 4 rows in St st (K, P, K, P).
Next row: P.
Then P, K, P, K, P.
On the next row unravel CO sts put them on a spare needle and k them together with the current row sts one by one.

For sizes 40, 42, 50 only. Start working on Diamond st patt chart immediately pertaining to your size. (starts on WS).

For all other sizes:
Purl WS row. Then start working on the Diamond st patt chart per-

taining to your size. For working patt from the chart pm after every patt repeat to ease the process. Work straight in patt for [142, 142, 142][142, 146, 146, 150][150, 150, 156] rows.

Armhole shaping

Continue working in Diamond st patt.
BO [3, 3, 4][4, 4, 4, 4][5, 5, 5] sts in the beg of next 2 rows.
BO [2, 2, 2][3, 3, 3, 3][3, 3, 3] sts in the beg of foll 2 rows.
Then continue to dec 1 st on each side every other row total of [6, 7, 8][8, 9, 11, 12][12, 13, 15] times.
Decrease in the foll manner: K1, k2tog, work in patt till last 3 sts, ssk, k1.

Continue working straight till you have worked [68, 70, 72][76, 78, 80, 82][86, 88, 90] rows/[6.75, 7, 7.25][7.5, 7.75, 8, 8.25] [8.5, 8.75, 9]in/[17, 18, 18.5][19, 19.5, 20.5, 21][21.5, 22, 23] cm from beg of armhole decreases.

AT THE SAME TIME
When you have worked [160, 160, 160][160, 163, 163, 168][168, 168, 173] rows of Diamond st patt from bottom of the body start V-neck shaping.

Left side front

Mark center st on your needle.
Row 1 (RS)(dec): Work to 2 sts before center st, ssk, m1. Turn.
Row 2 (WS): Work back in patt.
Place Right Side sts on stitch holder.
Continue working on Left Side sts dec 1 st at the end of every other row (RS) total of [25, 26, 27][28, 29, 30, 31][32, 33, 34] times.
[22, 23, 23][24, 25, 25, 26][27, 28, 28] sts place on stitch holder.

Right side front

Transfer sts from stitch holder onto needle. Rejoin yarn on RS.
Continue in Diamond st patt and continuing armhole shaping and AT THE SAME TIME perform V-neck shaping.
Row 1 (RS)(dec): K1, k2tog, work to end in patt.
Row 2 (WS): Work in patt.
Continue working on Right Side sts dec 1 st at the beg of every other row (RS) total of [25, 26, 27][28, 29, 30, 31][32, 33, 34] times.
[22, 23, 23][24, 25, 25, 26][27, 28, 28] sts place on stitch holder.

BACK

Work Back foll instructions same as for Front till armhole.

Armhole shaping

Continue working in Diamond st patt.

BO [3, 3, 4][4, 4, 4, 4][5, 5, 5] sts in the beg of next 2 rows.
BO [2, 2, 2][3, 3, 3, 3][3, 3, 3] sts in the beg of foll 2 rows.
Then continue to dec 1 st on each side every other row total of [6, 7, 8][8, 9, 11, 12][12, 13, 15] times.
Decrease in the foll manner: K1, k2tog, work in patt till last 3 sts, ssk, k1.

Continue working straight till you have worked [68, 70, 72] [76, 78, 80, 82][86, 88, 90] rows/[6.75, 7, 7.25][7.5, 7.75, 8, 8.25][8.5, 8.75, 9]in/[17, 18, 18.5][19, 19.5, 20.5, 21][21.5, 22, 23]cm from beg of armhole decreases. Leave sts on the needle.

ASSEMBLY

With both front and back facing WS join shoulders using 3-needle BO method.
[49, 51, 53][55, 57, 59, 61][63, 65, 67] center sts of the back leave on the needle. Rejoin yarn (1 strands only) on RS. P a row. Then continue working in St st for 8 rows.
RS: K.
WS: P.
BO loosely. Fold at p row and whip stitch it onto inside of the top. Worked only on the back.

ARMHOLE BANDS

At the arm's edge mark center of each shoulder, measure [3.75, 4, 4][4.25, 4.25, 4.5, 4.5][4.75, 4.75, 5]in/[9.5, 10, 10][11, 11, 11.5, 11.5][12, 12, 12.5]cm from the mark in each direction. Pm to indicate.

Using smaller needle pick up in rib patt [78, 84, 84][88, 88, 94, 94][98, 98, 104] sts.
Start working in double knitting by always sl first st of each row.
Row 1: Sl, *k1, slwyif,* , repeat from * to 1 st on the needle, k1.
Row 2: Sl, *k1, slwyif,* , repeat from * to 1 st on the needle, k1.
Work in established patt until it measures .75in/2cm. Take a second needle and separate sts of front and back. Graft (Kitchener Stitch).

FINISHING

Gently soak in warm water, do not wring. Lay flat to dry. While still damp press the pleats in place through ironing cloth. Let it dry completely. Mattress stitch sides together and weave in all ends.

[7.5, 7.75, 8.25][8.25, 8.75, 9, 9.5][9.75, 10, 10.25]in
[19, 19.5, 21][21.5, 22, 22.75, 24][24.75, 25.25, 26]cm

[3.5, 3.5, 3.5][3.75, 3.75, 3.75, 4][4.25, 4.25, 4.25]in
[8.75, 8.75, 8.75][9.5, 9.5, 9.5, 10][10.75, 10.75, 10.75]cm

[5.5, 5.75, 6]
[6.25, 6.5, 6.75, 7]
[7.25, 7.5, 7.75]in

[14, 14.5, 15]
[15.75, 16.5, 17, 17.75]
[18.25, 19, 19.5]cm

[6.75, 7, 7.25]
[7.5, 7.75, 8, 8.25]
[8.5, 8.75, 9]in

[17, 17.75, 18.25]
[19, 19.5, 20.25, 21]
[21.5, 22, 22.75]cm

[14.25, 14.25, 14.25]
[14.25, 14.5, 14.5, 15]
[15, 15, 15.5]in

[36, 36, 36]
[36, 36.75, 36.75, 38]
[38, 38, 39.25]cm

[16, 16, 16]
[16, 16.25, 16.25, 16.75]
[16.75, 16.75, 17.25]in

[40.5, 40.5, 40.5]
[40.5, 41.25, 41.25, 42.5]
[42.5, 42.5, 43.75]cm

[17.75, 18.5, 19.5][20.5, 21.5, 22.25, 23.25][24.25, 25, 26]in
[45, 47, 49.5][52, 54.5, 56.5, 59][61.5, 63.5, 66]cm

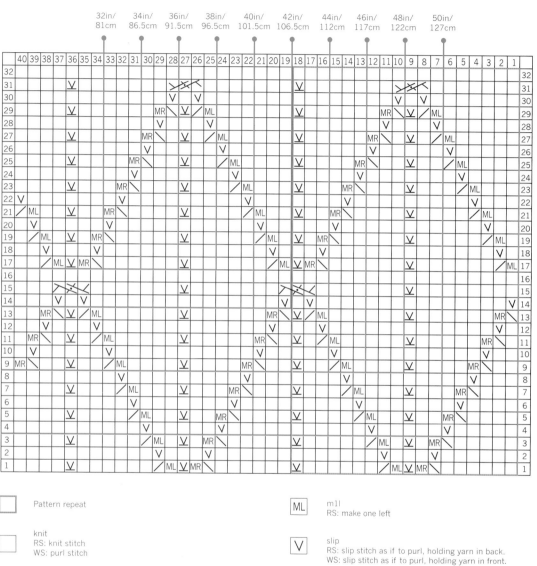

32in/ 81cm 34in/ 86.5cm 36in/ 91.5cm 38in/ 96.5cm 40in/ 101.5cm 42in/ 106.5cm 44in/ 112cm 46in/ 117cm 48in/ 122cm 50in/ 127cm

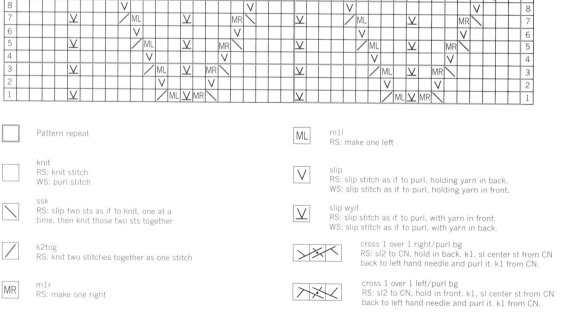

☐	Pattern repeat
☐	knit RS: knit stitch WS: purl stitch
╲	ssk RS: slip two sts as if to knit, one at a time, then knit those two sts together
╱	k2tog RS: knit two stitches together as one stitch
MR	m1r RS: make one right
ML	m1l RS: make one left
V	slip RS: slip stitch as if to purl, holding yarn in back. WS: slip stitch as if to purl, holding yarn in front.
V̲	slip wyif RS: slip stitch as if to purl, with yarn in front. WS: slip stitch as if to purl, with yarn in back.
⤬	cross 1 over 1 right/purl bg RS: sl2 to CN, hold in back. k1, sl center st from CN back to left hand needle and purl it. k1 from CN.
⤬	cross 1 over 1 left/purl bg RS: sl2 to CN, hold in front. k1, sl center st from CN back to left hand needle and purl it. k1 from CN.

TRAPEZIUM PULLOVER
ひし形の外套

Linen paper is a unique light weight fiber that creates
the organic drape seen in this pullover. Combine it with
lace cashmere and you have a fabric that is wearable
against bare skin. A flared silhouette, including continu-
ous body and sleeves construction, make it flattering
and easy to make, yet completely seamless. The bottom
edge is accented with a pair of elongated contrasting
pockets, while the neckline is enhanced with an array of
square metal buttons reminiscent of jewelry.

by OLGA BURAYA-KEFELIAN

SIZES
To fit bust size [32, 34, 36][38, 40, 42, 44][46, 48, 50]in/[81, 86.5, 91.5][96.5, 101.5, 106.5, 112][117, 122, 127]cm

Finished measurements [32, 34, 36][38, 40, 42, 44][46, 48, 50]in/[81, 86.5, 91.5][96.5, 101.5, 106.5, 112][117, 122, 127]cm

Length [21.25, 21.75, 22][22.5, 22.75, 23.25, 23.5][24, 24.5, 24.5]in/[54, 55, 56][57, 58, 59, 59.5][61, 62, 62]cm

YARN
Habu Textiles A-60 shosenshi paper, 100% linen; 280yds(250m)/1 oz(28gr); 115 (beige)
[3, 3, 4][4, 4, 4, 4][4, 5, 5]oz/[78, 82, 87] [92, 97, 102, 107] [111, 116, 121]g
OR
[772, 820, 869][917, 965, 1013, 1062][1110, 1158, 1206]yds/ [690, 733, 777][820, 863, 906, 949][992, 1035, 1078]m

Habu Textiles A-34 2/26 cashmere; 100% cashmere; 404yds(368m)/1 oz(28gr); 1305 (lime)
[2, 2, 2.5][2.5, 2.5, 3, 3][3, 3, 3.5]oz/[56, 56, 70][70, 70, 84, 84] [84, 84, 98]g
OR
[760, 808, 856][904, 951, 999, 1046][1093, 1141, 1189]yds/ [693, 736, 780][823, 866, 910, 953][996, 1040, 1083]m

NEEDLES
4 mm 24in circular
4 mm dpns, set of 5 (or size to obtain gauge)

NOTIONS
Stitch markers
Stitch holders
Crochet hook
Scrap yarn
2 row counters
Darning needle
8 x .5in square buttons (optional)

GAUGE
22 sts and 32 rows in 4in/10cm over washed and blocked St st swatch knit in a round with both yarns held together

NOTES
This pullover is worked by carrying 1 strand of each yarn together throughout the body. Pockets and neckline trim are worked by holding 2 strands of A-60 shosenshi paper together.

BODY

Using circular needle CO [220, 232, 242][254, 264, 276, 286] [298, 308, 320] sts.
Join in a round, carefully not to twist, pm to indicate beg of a round.
Slm, k [110, 116, 121][127, 132, 138, 143][149, 154, 160], pm, k [110, 116, 121][127, 132, 138, 143][149, 154, 160].
Work straight around in St st for 9 rnds.
Decrease rnd: Slm, k1, ssk, k to last 3 sts before next m, k2tog, k1, slm, k1, ssk, k to last 3 sts before next m, k2tog, k1.
Work previous 10 rnds total of 11 times. [176, 188, 198][210, 220, 232, 242][254, 264, 276] sts.
Then work [0, 0, 0][2, 2, 4, 4][6, 8, 8] rnds straight.
Body will measure [13.75, 13.75, 13.75][14, 14, 14.25, 14.25] [14.5, 14.75, 14.75]in/[35, 35, 35][35.5, 35.5, 36, 36] [37, 37.5, 37.5]cm from CO edge.

AT THE SAME TIME

When body measures [3, 3, 3][3.25, 3.25, 3.5, 3.5][3.75, 4, 4] in/[7.5, 7.5, 7.5][8.5, 8.5, 9, 9][9.5, 10, 10]cm or [24, 24, 24] [26, 26, 28, 28][30, 32, 32] rnds from CO edge make pocket openings.
Slm, k [12, 12, 13][13, 14, 14, 15][15, 16, 16] sts with Main yarn, k [19, 20, 21][22, 23, 24, 25][26, 27, 28] sts with scrap yarn, sl those sts worked with scrap yarn back onto the left needle and work across them with Main yarn, k [44, 48, 49][53, 54, 58, 59][61, 62, 66] sts, k [19, 20, 21][22, 23, 24, 25][26, 27, 28] sts with scrap yarn, sl those sts worked with scrap yarn back onto the left needle and work them now with Main yarn, k [12, 12, 13][13, 14, 14, 15][15, 16, 16] sts, slm, k to end of the rnd. Continue in patt.

FRONT AND SLEEVES

From this point pullover is worked flat.
K to next m, using Provisional CO method with crochet hook and scrap yarn CO [38, 38, 38][38, 38, 44, 44][44, 46, 46] sts onto left needle. K across those CO sts in Main yarn. Turn. P back across to other m, then using Provisional CO method with crochet hook and scrap yarn CO [38, 38, 38][38, 38, 44, 44][44, 46, 46] sts onto left needle, p across those sts. Turn. Place back sts on stitch holder. [164, 170, 175][181, 186, 204, 209][215, 224, 230] sts on the needle.

Work straight in St st until it measures [4.75, 5, 5.25][5.5, 5.75, 6, 6.25][6.5, 6.75, 7]in/[12, 12.5, 13.5][14, 14.5, 15, 16] [16.5, 17, 18]cm from sleeve CO edge and start front neckline shaping.

BO center [10, 12, 13][13, 14, 14, 15][15, 16, 20] sts.
Continue working on Right Front decreasing 2 sts every other row on the neckline edge total of [7, 8, 8][8, 8, 8, 8][8, 8, 7]

times. Finish working Right Front and place all sts on a stitch holder.

Rejoin yarn on the WS onto Left Front and decrease 2 sts every other row on the neckline edge total of [7, 8, 8][8, 8, 8, 8] [8, 8, 7] times.
Finish working Left Front and place all sts on a stitch holder. [38, 44, 45][45, 46, 46, 47][47, 48, 48] sts decreased for neckline total.

AT THE SAME TIME

When front measures [5.75, 6, 6.25][6.5, 6.75, 7, 7.25][7.5, 7.75, 8]in/[14.5, 15, 16][16.5, 17, 18, 18.5][19, 19.5, 20.5]cm start short row shoulder shaping.
K to [14, 14, 16][17, 13, 14, 16][11, 15, 18] sts of the row, sl next st, w&t. Turn and work back.
Continue w&t distancing [6, 6, 6][7, 8, 8, 8][9, 9, 9] sts from a previous wrap total of 8 times on each side.
Next row: K picking up all wraps and k them tog with the sts they are wrapped around.

Put all sts on scrap yarn or stitch holders.

BACK

Transfer sts from stitch holder onto the needle.
Unravel CO from each sleeve and place sts onto the same needle. With RS facing rejoin yarn and work in St st for [5.75, 6, 6.25][6.5, 6.75, 7, 7.25][7.5, 7.75, 8]in/[14.5, 15, 16][16.5, 17, 18, 18.5][19, 19.5, 20.5]cm from the sleeve CO edge.
Start short row shoulder shaping.
K to [14, 14, 16][11, 13, 14, 16][11, 15, 18] sts of the row, sl next st, w&t. Turn work and work back.
Continue w&t distancing [6, 6, 6][7, 7, 8, 8][9, 9, 9] sts from a previous wrap total of 8 times on each side.
Next row: K picking up all wraps and k them tog with the sts they are wrapped around.

AT THE SAME TIME

When back measures [7, 7.25, 7.5][7.75, 8, 8.25, 8.5][8.75, 9, 9.25]in/[18, 18.5, 19][19.5, 20.5, 21, 21.5][22, 23, 23.5]cm start back neckline shaping.
BO center [26, 32, 33][33, 34, 34, 35][35, 36, 36] sts.
Then continue working on Right Back side only and decreasing 2 sts every other row on neckline edge total of 3 times.
Break yarn and place all sts on a stitch holder.

Rejoin yarn on WS of Left Back side on the neckline edge and decrease 2 sts every other row total of 3 times.
Break yarn and place all sts on a stitch holder.
[38, 44, 45][45, 46, 46, 47][47, 48, 48] sts decreased for neckline total.

ASSEMBLY

Place right sleeve sts and left sleeve sts on needles and Graft (Kitchener Stitch) shoulders together. Repeat for the other sleeve. With 2 strands of A-60 and dpns pick up [76, 88, 90][90, 92, 92, 94][94, 96, 96] sts around the neckline and p around. K next round. BO loosely in p.

POCKETS

Carefully remove scrap yarn of each pocket and put [24, 24, 26][26, 28, 28, 30][30, 32, 32] sts evenly on dpns. Take 2 strands of A-60 and p around. Pm to indicate beg of a rnd.
Work in St st for [4.5, 4.5, 4.5][4.75, 4.75, 5, 5][5.25, 5.25, 5.5]in/[11.5, 11.5, 11.5][12, 12, 12.5, 12.5][13.5, 13.5, 14]cm. Fold the pockets flat to accommodate the pullover shape, divide sts between 2 needles and Graft (Kitchener Stitch) the pocket shut. (Optional · arrange buttons along the neckline, pin and sew in place.)

FINISHING

Wash gently in lukewarm water, do not wring. Lightly block and lay flat to dry. Once dry fold 2in/5cm cuffs on each sleeve and sew in place.

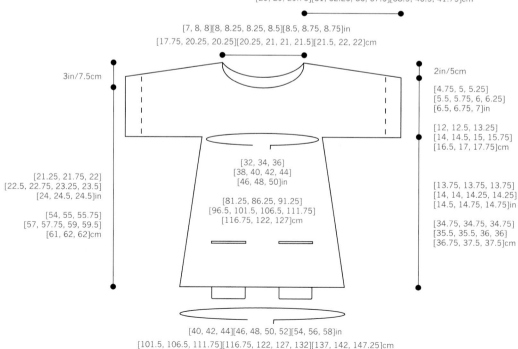

[11.5, 11.5, 11.75][12.25, 12.75, 14.25, 14.75][15. 25, 16, 16.5]in
[29, 29, 29.75][31, 32.25, 36, 37.5][38.5, 40.5, 41.75]cm

[7, 8, 8][8, 8.25, 8.25, 8.5][8.5, 8.75, 8.75]in
[17.75, 20.25, 20.25][20.25, 21, 21, 21.5][21.5, 22, 22]cm

3in/7.5cm

2in/5cm

[4.75, 5, 5.25]
[5.5, 5.75, 6, 6.25]
[6.5, 6.75, 7]in

[12, 12.5, 13.25]
[14, 14.5, 15, 15.75]
[16.5, 17, 17.75]cm

[21.25, 21.75, 22]
[22.5, 22.75, 23.25, 23.5]
[24, 24.5, 24.5]in

[54, 55, 55.75]
[57, 57.75, 59, 59.5]
[61, 62, 62]cm

[32, 34, 36]
[38, 40, 42, 44]
[46, 48, 50]in

[81.25, 86.25, 91.25]
[96.5, 101.5, 106.5, 111.75]
[116.75, 122, 127]cm

[13.75, 13.75, 13.75]
[14, 14, 14.25, 14.25]
[14.5, 14.75, 14.75]in

[34.75, 34.75, 34.75]
[35.5, 35.5, 36, 36]
[36.75, 37.5, 37.5]cm

[40, 42, 44][46, 48, 50, 52][54, 56, 58]in
[101.5, 106.5, 111.75][116.75, 122, 127, 132][137, 142, 147.25]cm

chapter two

SUBTLE LAYERS

 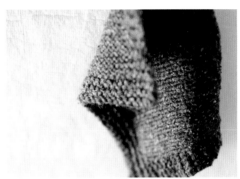

DUPLICITY PULLOVER
レイヤープル

The deceptively simple construction of this seamless raglan pullover renders interest and style in this thoroughly modern garment. Two contrasting yarns are worked into creating intriguing texture, akin to a doubled layer fabric. The clever details are emphasized with transparency and bright color, while texture variation provides a wonderfully up-to-date layered look. Suitable for office or casual weekend · a design piece perfect for every occasion.

by OLGA BURAYA-KEFELIAN

To fit bust size [32, 34, 36][38, 40, 42, 44][46, 48, 50]in/[81.5, 86.5, 91.5][96.5, 101.5, 106.5, 112][117, 122, 127]cm

Finished measurements [34, 36, 38][40, 42, 44, 46][48, 50, 52] in/[86.5, 91.5, 96.5][101.5, 106.5, 112, 117][122, 127, 132]cm

Length (measured from lower hem) [23, 23.5, 24][24.5, 25, 25.5, 26][26.5, 27, 27.5]in/[58.5, 59.5, 61][62, 63.5, 65, 66] [67.5, 68.5, 70]cm

YARN
Habu Textiles A-1 2/17 tsumugi silk, 100% silk; 265yds(239m)/ oz(28g); 54 (cafe) Main yarn
[6, 6, 6.5][7, 7.5, 7.5, 8][8.5, 8.5, 9]oz/[159, 168, 178][188, 198, 208, 218][228, 238, 248]g
OR
[1497, 1590, 1684][1778, 1871, 1965, 2058][2152, 2245, 2339] yds/[1351, 1434, 1519][1604, 1688, 1773, 1857][1940, 2025, 2110]m
Worked with 2 strands held together

Habu Textiles A-148 1/17.6 wool stainless steel, 75% wool, 25% stainless steel; 547yds(492m)/oz(28 g); 45 (terra cotta) Contrasting yarn
[1, 1, 1.5][1.5, 1.5, 1.5, 1.5][1.5, 1.5, 2]oz/[27, 28, 30][32, 33, 35, 37][38, 40, 42]g
OR
[515, 547, 580][612, 644, 676, 708][741, 773, 805]yds/[464, 492, 522][551, 580, 609, 637][667, 696, 725]m
Worked with 2 strands held together

NEEDLES
3.75 mm 16in, 24in circular
3.75 mm dpns, set of 5 (or size to obtain gauge)

NOTIONS
Stitch markers
Stitch holders
Row counter
Tapestry needle

GAUGE
20 sts and 32 rows in 4in/10cm over washed and blocked St st swatch knit in a round with 2 strands of Main yarn held together

BODY

Using 2 strands of Main yarn and longer circular needle CO [202, 212, 222][232, 242, 252, 262][272, 282, 292] sts.
Join in a round, pm to indicate beg of a rnd, k [101, 106, 111] [116, 121, 126, 131][136, 141, 146], pm, k [101, 106, 111] [116, 121, 126, 131][136, 141, 146] sts.

Bust shaping

K [11, 12, 12][12, 12, 13, 13][13, 13, 14] rnds straight.
Dec rnd: Slm, k2tog, k to 2 sts before next m, ssk, slm, k2tog, k to 2 sts before next m, ssk.
Work previous [12, 13, 13][13, 13, 14, 14][14, 14, 15] rnds total of 8 times.
[170, 180, 190][200, 210, 220, 230][240, 250, 260] sts on the needle. Put aside and work on sleeves.

SLEEVES

(make 2)
Using 2 strands of Main yarn and dpns CO [66, 66, 71][75, 81, 84, 85][86, 90, 92] sts. Join in a rnd, pm to indicate beg of a rnd.

Work [22, 23, 23][24, 25, 25, 26][27, 27, 28] rnds straight.
Dec rnd: Slm, k2tog, work around to 2 sts before m, ssk.
Work previous [23, 24, 24][25, 26, 26, 27][28, 28, 29] rnds total of 3 times.

Then work [1, 0, 2][1, 0, 2, 1][0, 2, 1] rnds straight. [60, 60, 65] [69, 75, 78, 79][80, 84, 86] sts. Transfer sts on stitch holders. Make second sleeve.

YOKE

Count [10, 10, 12][14, 17, 19, 19][20, 22, 23] center sts on each sleeve and place those sts on stitch holders.
Count [10, 10, 13][15, 18, 19, 20][20, 22, 23] center sts from each side of the body and place those sts on stitch holders.
K all remaining sts pertaining to the front of the pullover, pm, then transfer sts of the right sleeve onto the left needle and k across them, pm, then k across back sts, pm, slip and k across left sleeve sts, pm to indicate beg of your yoke rnds.
[250, 260, 270][280, 290, 300, 310][320, 330, 340] sts.
Work [11, 10, 9][8, 7, 6, 5][4, 3, 2] rnds straight.

Raglan shaping

Work 2 rnds.
Dec rnd: *Slm, k2, ssk, k to 4 sts before next m, k2tog, k2*.
Repeat from * throughout the round.
Repeat previous 3 rnds total of [17, 18, 19][20, 21, 22, 23][24, 25, 26] times total.

[114, 116, 118][120, 122, 124, 126][128, 130, 132] sts rem.
After last rnd of raglan shaping is complete:

Row 1: K to back's m, slm, k across till 5 sts before next m, sl next st, w&t.
Row 2: P back to 5 sts before next m, sl next st, w&t.
Row 3: K to 5 sts before previous wrap, sl next st, w&t.
Row 4: P to 5 sts before previous wrap, sl next st, w&t.
On the next rnd. Work around picking up and k all wraps together with the sts they are wrapped around.

Collar

P 1 rnd.
K 16 rnds and BO loosely.

FINISHING

Take 2 strands of Contrasting yarn and with a shorter circular needle and RS facing, pick up and knit around on the inside of the collar (just 1 row below that purl round) into every st. [114, 116, 118][120, 122, 124, 126][128, 130, 132] sts.
Work for 3.5in/9cm in St st. BO loosely.

Turn sleeve hem outside, measure 1in/2.5cm from sleeve's edge and with 2 strands of Contrasting yarn and dpns (or two circulars) pick up and k [65, 66, 71][75, 81, 84, 85][86, 90, 92] sts on the inside.
Work for 5in/12.5cm in St st. BO loosely.
Repeat for second sleeve.

Turn the pullover's hem outside, measure 1in/2.5cm from edge and with 2 strands of Contrasting yarn and longer circular needle pick up and knit [202, 212, 222][232, 242, 252, 262] [272, 282, 292] sts on the inside. Work in St st for 3.5in/9cm. BO loosely.

Transfer sts from a sleeve and side of the body on 2 needles and Graft (Kitchener stitch) them together. Repeat for other side.

Weave in all ends. Soak in warm water, lightly block and lay flat to dry.

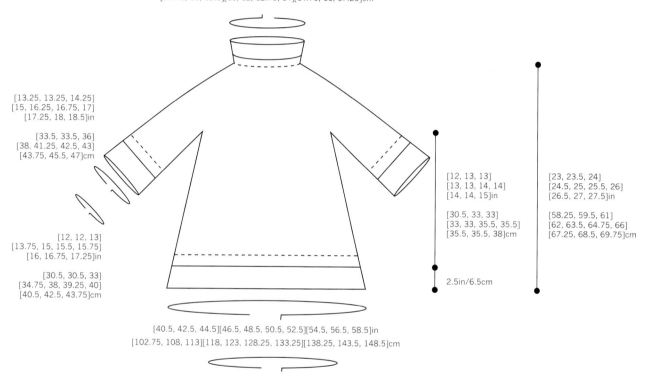

[22.75, 23.25, 23.5][24, 24.5, 24.75, 25.25][25.5, 26, 26.5]in
[57.75, 59, 59.5][61, 62, 62.75, 64][64.75, 66, 67.25]cm

[13.25, 13.25, 14.25]
[15, 16.25, 16.75, 17]
[17.25, 18, 18.5]in

[33.5, 33.5, 36]
[38, 41.25, 42.5, 43]
[43.75, 45.5, 47]cm

[12, 12, 13]
[13.75, 15, 15.5, 15.75]
[16, 16.75, 17.25]in

[30.5, 30.5, 33]
[34.75, 38, 39.25, 40]
[40.5, 42.5, 43.75]cm

[12, 13, 13]
[13, 13, 14, 14]
[14, 14, 15]in

[30.5, 33, 33]
[33, 33, 35.5, 35.5]
[35.5, 35.5, 38]cm

[23, 23.5, 24]
[24.5, 25, 25.5, 26]
[26.5, 27, 27.5]in

[58.25, 59.5, 61]
[62, 63.5, 64.75, 66]
[67.25, 68.5, 69.75]cm

2.5in/6.5cm

[40.5, 42.5, 44.5][46.5, 48.5, 50.5, 52.5][54.5, 56.5, 58.5]in
[102.75, 108, 113][118, 123, 128.25, 133.25][138.25, 143.5, 148.5]cm

[34, 36, 38][40, 42, 44, 46][48, 50, 52]in
[86.5, 91.5, 96.5][101.5, 106.5, 111, 117][122, 127, 132]cm

ARCUS PULLOVER
アーチ雲プルオーバー

Cocoon yourself in this luxurious transformable pullover. Worked continuously in a tube with a whisper soft
silk mohair yarn blend, this project will keep hands and
spirit happy. Whether decoratively gathered along the
shoulder to create cascading folds around the yoke, or
stretched into an over sized cowl around the neck, or
worn as a snood over your head · this design gives you
ultimate flexibility and possibility for experimentation.

by OLGA BURAYA·KEFELIAN

SIZES

To fit bust size [32, 34, 36][38, 40, 42, 44][46, 48, 50]in/[81.5, 86.5, 91.5][96.5, 101.5, 106.5, 111][117, 122, 127]cm

Finished measurements [32, 34, 36][38, 40, 42, 44][46, 48, 50]in/[81, 86.5, 91.5][96.5, 101.5, 106.5, 112][117, 122, 127]cm

Length to underarm [14.75, 15, 15][15.25, 15.25, 15.25, 15.25][15.75, 15.75, 16]in/[37.5, 38, 38][38.5, 38.5, 39.5, 39.5][40, 40, 40.5]cm

YARN

Habu Textiles A-32B 1/12 silk mohair, 60% silk, 40% mohair; 373 yds(335m)/oz(28g); 64 (bamboo green)
[2.5, 2.5, 2.5][2.5, 3, 3, 3][3.5, 3.5, 3.5]oz/[60, 63, 66][70, 74, 77, 81][85, 88, 92]g
OR
[800, 832, 880][935, 986, 1027, 1080][1134, 1174, 1227]yds/[718, 755, 790][838, 886, 922, 970][1018, 1054, 1102]m

NEEDLES

3.75 mm 24in circular and dpns, set of 5
3.5 mm dpns, set of 5 (or size to obtain gauge)

NOTIONS

1 stitch marker in color A
1 stitch marker in color B
4 stitch markers in color C
2 row counters
Scrap yarn
Crochet hook
Tapestry needle

GAUGE

24 sts and 36 rows in 4in/10cm over washed and blocked St st in the round on bigger needle

BODY

Using Cable method CO [204, 216, 228][240, 252, 264, 276][288, 300, 312] sts.
Join in a round and pm with color A at the join. P [102, 108, 114][120, 126, 132, 138][144, 150, 156] sts, pm color B to indicate other side seam, p [102, 108, 114][120, 126, 132, 138][144, 150, 156] sts.
Purl 5 more rnds. Switch to St st for the rest of the body.
Work [2, 4, 4][0, 0, 1, 1][2, 2, 4] rnds even.

Hip decreases

Dec rnd: Slm, k2, ssk, k to 4 sts before next m, k2tog, k2, slm, k2, ssk, k to 4 sts before next m, k2tog, k2.
Work 4 rnds straight. Repeat the last 5 rnds a total of 12 times.
Work [2, 2, 2][0, 0, 1, 1][2, 2, 2] rnds straight for the waist.

Bust increases

Work [6, 6, 6][7, 7, 7, 7][7, 7, 7] rnds even.
Inc rnd: Slm, k2, m1, k to 2 sts before next m, m1, k2, slm, k2, m1, k to 2 sts before next m, m1, k2.
Repeat the last [7, 7, 7][8, 8, 8, 8][8, 8, 8] rnds a total of 9 times.
[192, 204, 216][228, 240, 252, 264][276, 288, 300] sts.

SLEEVES

Transfer [13, 14, 15][15, 16, 19, 20][21, 22, 23] sts from each underarm to scrap yarn.
[166, 176, 186][198, 208, 214, 224][234, 244, 254] sts rem.

On the next rnd, using scrap yarn and crochet hook Provisionally CO over each underarm gap [36, 38, 40][44, 48, 50, 52][56, 58, 62] sts for sleeves, replacing color A and B markers in the middle of each CO section. Continue in Main yarn.
[238, 252, 266][286, 304, 314, 328][346, 360, 378] sts.

YOKE

Set up rnd: Slm A, k5, pm color C, knit to 5 sts before B marker, pm color C, k5, slm B, k5, pm color C, k to last 5 sts, pm color C, k5 to first marker A.

DRAWSTRING CASINGS

(2 rnd repeat)
Begin working the integrated drawstring casings as follows:
Rnd 1: Slm A, k2, sl1kwise wyif, k1, sl1kwise wyif, slm C, work to next m C, slm C, k1, sl1kwise wyif, k1, sl1kwise wyif, k1, slm B, k2, sl1kwise wyif, k1, sl1kwise wyif, slm C, work to next m C, slm C, k1, sl1kwise wyif, k1, sl1kwise wyif, k1.

Rnd 2: Slm A, k1, sl1kwise wyib, p1, sl1kwise wyib, p1, slm C, work to next m C, slm C, sl1kwise wyib, p1, sl1kwise wyib, p1, k1, slm B, k1, sl1kwise wyib, k1, sl1kwise wyib, p1, slm C, work

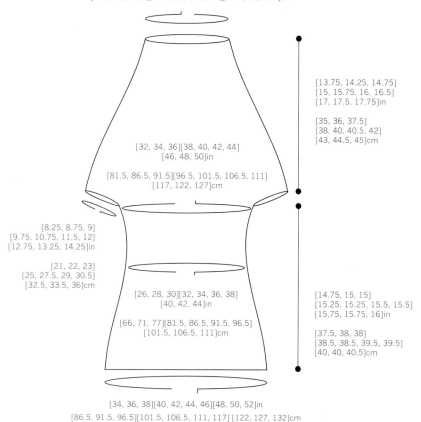

[23.75, 23.25, 23][23.75, 24.75, 25, 25.25][25.75, 26, 25.75]in
[60.5, 59, 58.5][60.5, 63, 63.5, 64][65.5, 66, 65.5]cm

[13.75, 14.25, 14.75]
[15, 15.75, 16, 16.5]
[17, 17.5, 17.75]in

[35, 36, 37.5]
[38, 40, 40.5, 42]
[43, 44.5, 45]cm

[32, 34, 36][38, 40, 42, 44]
[46, 48, 50]in

[81.5, 86.5, 91.5][96.5, 101.5, 106.5, 111]
[117, 122, 127]cm

[8.25, 8.75, 9]
[9.75, 10.75, 11.5, 12]
[12.75, 13.25, 14.25]in

[21, 22, 23]
[25, 27.5, 29, 30.5]
[32.5, 33.5, 36]cm

[26, 28, 30][32, 34, 36, 38]
[40, 42, 44]in

[66, 71, 77][81.5, 86.5, 91.5, 96.5]
[101.5, 106.5, 111]cm

[14.75, 15, 15]
[15.25, 15.25, 15.5, 15.5]
[15.75, 15.75, 16]in

[37.5, 38, 38]
[38.5, 38.5, 39.5, 39.5]
[40, 40, 40.5]cm

[34, 36, 38][40, 42, 44, 46][48, 50, 52]in
[86.5, 91.5, 96.5][101.5, 106.5, 111, 117] [122, 127, 132]cm

to next m C, slm C, sl1kwise wyib, p1, sl1kwise wyib, p1, k1.
Continue working yoke in St st and rep previous 2 rnds for draw-string casings throughout the entire yoke.

AT THE SAME TIME work yoke decreases

Yoke decreases
Work [4, 3, 3][2, 2, 2, 2][2, 2, 2] rnds even.
Dec rnd: *Slm A, work casing (5 sts), slm C, k1, ssk, work to 3 sts before next m C, k2tog, k1, work casing (5 sts); rep from* once more.
Repeat previous [5, 4, 4][3, 3, 3, 3][3, 3, 3] rnds a total of [24,

28, 32][36, 39, 41, 44][48, 51, 56] times.
[142, 140, 138][142, 148, 150, 152][154, 156, 154] sts rem.
Work even for [0, 12, 0][22, 19, 17, 12] [4, 0, 0] rnds. Purl 3 rnds.
Loosely BO all sts purlwise.

FINISHING
Unravel CO from the cap sleeve and distribute sts over 2 larger dpns; place underarm sts from scrap yarn on another dpn and pm in the middle of that needle to indicate beg of rnd. Join yarn and purl 4 rnds. Loosely BO all sts purlwise. Repeat for the other sleeve.

I-cords (make 2)
Using smaller dpns CO 5 sts.
Knit across, slide sts to the beginning of the needle. Repeat from *.
Work in the same manner till I-cord measures [36, 36, 36][40, 40, 40, 40][42, 42, 42]in/[91.5, 91.5, 91.5][101.5, 101.5, 101.5, 101.5][111, 111, 111]cm. BO all sts.

Weave in all ends. Wash and block lightly. Take small safety pin and pin it onto 1 end of the I-cord, starting from the bottom of the cap sleeve feed it up through first track of the drawstring casing, trying carefully to separate sts belonging to back and front (you may find it easier to accomplish by turning the garment inside out). Once at the neck, turn and feed I-cord down through second track of the casing. Tie small knots on the ends of the I-cord. Distribute fullness evenly and tie cord in a bow. Repeat the same on the other side. Adjust as desired.

PUZZLE VEST
パズルベスト

Constructed out of 3 pieces, this puzzle is easily put together. Each of them is knit in a separate chevron pattern to create texture and visually entertain the knitter as well as onlooker. Contrasting colors translate this deconstructed vest into a fun garment to wear and own. Layer it with a sleeved shirt or wear it individually, it would make any outfit unique.

by OLGA BURAYA·KEFELIAN

SIZES

To fit bust size [32, 34, 36][38, 40, 42, 44][46, 48, 50]in/[81.5, 86.5, 91.5][96.5, 101.5, 106.5, 111][117, 122, 127]cm

Finished measurements [34, 36, 38][40, 42, 44, 46][48, 50, 52] in/[86.5, 91.5, 96.5][101.5, 106.5, 111, 117][122, 127, 132]cm

Length [18.25, 18.75, 19.25][19.75, 20.25, 20.75, 21.25][21.75, 22.25, 22.75]in/[46.5, 47.5, 48.5][50, 51.5, 52.5, 54][55, 56.5, 58]cm

YARN

Habu Textiles A·1 2/17 tsumugi silk, 100% silk; 265yds(239m)/ oz(28g); 44 (blue) (MC)
[4.6, 4.9, 5.1][5.4, 5.7, 6, 6.3][6.6, 6.9, 7.2]oz/[128, 136, 143] [151, 159, 167, 175][183, 191, 199]g
OR
[1202, 1277, 1352][1428, 1503, 1578, 1653][1728, 1803, 1878] yds/ [1084, 1152, 1219][1287, 1355, 1423, 1490][1558, 1626, 1694]m
Worked with 2 strands held together

42 (chocolate) (CC) [3.1, 3.3, 3.4][3.7, 3.9, 4, 4.3][4.4, 4.6, 4.8]oz/[86, 91, 96][102, 107, 112, 118][123, 128, 134]g
OR
[801, 851, 901][952, 1002, 1052, 1102][1152, 1202, 1252] yds/[723, 768, 813][859, 904, 949, 994][1039, 1084, 1130]m
Worked with 2 strands held together

NEEDLES

3.5 mm 24in circular
3.25 mm 24in circular
3.25 mm dpns, set of 5 (or size to obtain gauge)

NOTIONS

15 or 17 buttons
Stitch holders
Tapestry needle

GAUGE

24 sts and 36 rows in 4in/10cm over washed and blocked Chevron Stitch pattern (any variation) on larger needle with 2 strands held together

TWISTED RIB

Multiple of 2 sts
Row 1: *K1tbl, p1tbl* to end.
Rep Row 1.

Multiple of 2 sts + 1
Row 1: *K1tbl, p1tbl* to last st, k1tbl.
Row 2: *P1tbl, k1tbl* to last st, p1tbl.

SMALL CHEVRON PATTERN (8 stitch repeat over 8 rows)
R1 (RS): *P1, k7*.
R2 (WS): *K1, p5, k2*.
R3: *P3, k3, p2*.
R4: *K3, p1, k4*.
R5: *K1, p7*.
R6: *P1, k5, p2*.
R7: *K3, p3, k2*.
R8: *P3, k1, p4*.

MEDIUM CHEVRON PATTERN (6 stitch repeat over 12 rows)
R1 (RS): *P1, k5*.
R2 (WS): *P5, k1*.
R3: *P2, k3, p1*.
R4: *K1, p3, k2*.
R5: *P3, k1, p2*.
R6: *K2, p1, k3*.
R7: *K1, p5*.
R8: *K5, p1*.
R9: *K2, p3, k1*.
R10: *P1, k3, p2*.
R11: *K3, p1, k2*.
R12: *P2, k1, p3*.

LARGE CHEVRON PATTERN (8 stitch repeat over 16 rows)
R1 (RS): *K7, p1*.
R2 (WS): *K1, p7*.
R3: *P1, k5, p2*.
R4: *K2, p5, k1*.
R5: *P2, k3, p3*.
R6: *K3, p3, k2*.
R7: *P3, k1, p4*.
R8: *K4, p1, k3*.
R9: *P7, k1*.
R10: *P1, k7*.
R11: *K1, p5, k2*.
R12: *P2, k5, p1*.
R13: *K2, p3, k3*.
R14: *P3, k3, k2*.
R15: *K3, p1, k4*.
R16: *P4, k1, p3*.

BODY
Back and left front
(worked together)
Using 2 strands of CC and smaller needle CO [126, 135, 144] [152, 161, 169, 178][186, 195, 203] sts.
Work in Twisted Rib for 1.75in/4.5cm.
Switch to larger needle and 2 strands of MC and work in Small Chevron pattern until piece measures [11.25, 11.5, 11.75][12, 12.25, 12.5, 12.75][13, 13.25, 13.5]in/[27.5, 28, 30][30.5, 31, 32, 32.5][33, 33.5, 34.5]cm, ending with a WS row.

Armhole shaping
With RS facing, place the last (leftmost) [24, 27, 30][32, 35, 37, 40][42, 45, 47] sts on a holder for Upper left front.
Remaining [102, 108, 114][120, 126, 132, 138][144, 150, 156] sts form the Back.
Continue working in Small Chevron pattern and at the same time shape armholes as foll:
BO [4, 4, 4][5, 5, 5, 6][6, 6, 7] sts at beg of next 2 rows.
BO [2, 3, 3][2, 3, 3, 3][4, 4, 4] sts at beg of foll 2 rows.
Dec 1 st at each end of every RS row [6, 7, 8][9, 10, 11, 12][12, 13, 14] times in the foll manner: Ssk, work to last 2 sts, k2tog. [78, 80, 84][88, 90, 94, 96][100, 104, 106] sts.

Work even until armholes measure [7, 7.25, 7.5][7.75, 8, 8.25, 8.5][8.75, 9, 9.25]in/[18, 18.5, 19][19.5, 20, 20.5, 21][22, 23, 23.5]cm. Place all sts on a stitch holder.

Upper left front
Replace the [24, 27, 30][32, 35, 37, 40][42, 45, 47] held sts on needle. Rejoin yarn on the RS, continue in Small Chevron pattern and at the same time shape armhole as foll:
BO [4, 4, 4][5, 5, 5, 6][6, 6, 7] sts at beg of next row (RS).
Work 1 and all WS rows in patt.
BO [2, 3, 3][2, 3, 3, 3][4, 4, 4] sts at beg of foll row.
Dec 1 st at beg of every RS row [6, 7, 8][9, 10, 11, 12][12, 13, 14] times in the foll manner: Ssk, work to end. [12, 13, 15][16, 17, 18, 19][20, 22, 22] sts.

Work even until armhole measures [7, 7.25, 7.5][7.75, 8, 8.25, 8.5][8.75, 9, 9.25]in/[18, 18.5, 19][19.5, 20, 20.5, 21][22, 23, 23.5]cm. Place all sts on a stitch holder.

Center front
Using 2 strands of CC and smaller needle CO [72, 75, 78] [82, 85, 89, 92][96, 99, 103] sts. Work in Twisted Rib for 1.75in/4.5cm.

Switch to larger needle and 2 strands of MC and work in Large Chevron pattern until piece measures [6.25, 6.5, 6.75][7, 7.25, 7.5, 7.75][8, 8.25, 8.5]in/[16, 16.5, 17][18, 18.5, 19, 19.5]

[20.5, 21, 21.5]cm, ending with a RS row. Shape left side as foll:
Row 1 (WS): BO [8, 8, 8][8, 10, 10, 10][11, 12, 12] sts, work to end.
Row 2 and all RS rows: Work even in patt.
Row 3: BO [5, 5, 5][5, 5, 5, 7] [7, 8, 8] sts, work to end.
Row 5: BO 3 sts, work to end.
Rows 7, 9, 11: BO 2 sts, work to end.
Row 13: BO 1 st, work to end.

Continue to BO 1 st at beg of every WS row [7, 10, 13][15, 16, 18, 19][20, 21, 23] times more. [42, 42, 42][44, 44, 46, 46][48, 48, 50] sts.

Work even until Center front measures [14, 14.5, 15][15.5, 16, 16.5, 17][17.5, 18, 18.5]in/[35.5, 37, 38][39.5, 40.5, 42, 43] [44.5, 45.5, 47]cm from CO edge.
Switch to smaller needle and 2 strands of CC and work 8 rows in Twisted St Rib patt. BO loosely in rib.

Right front
Using 2 strands of MC and larger needle CO [2, 2, 2][2, 4, 4, 4] [5, 6, 6] sts. Work in Medium Chevron Stitch patt.
Row 1 and all RS rows: Work even.
Using Backward Loop method CO at the end of each WS row as foll:
Row 2 (WS): CO [5, 5, 5][5, 5, 5, 7][7, 8, 8] sts.
Row 4: CO 3 sts.
Rows 6, 8, 10: CO 2 sts.
Row 12: CO 1 st.
Continue to CO 1 st at beg of every WS row [7, 10, 13][15, 16, 18, 19][20, 21, 23] times more.

AT THE SAME TIME
When Right front measures 4in/10cm from CO edge ending with a RS row, shape armhole as foll:
BO [4, 4, 4][5, 5, 5, 6][6, 6, 7] sts at beg of next row (WS).
Work 1 RS row even.
BO [2, 3, 3][2, 3, 3, 3][4, 4, 4] sts at beg of next row.
Dec 1 st at end of every RS row [6, 7, 8][9, 10, 11, 12][12, 13, 14] times in the foll manner: Work to last 2 sts, k2tog. [12, 13, 15][16, 17, 18, 19][20, 22, 22] sts.

Work even until armhole measures [7, 7.25, 7.5][7.75, 8, 8.25, 8.5][8.75, 9, 9.25]in/[18, 18.5, 19][19.5, 20, 20.5, 21][22, 23, 23.5]cm. Place all sts on holder.

FINISHING
With RS facing using smaller needle and 2 strands of CC, pick up and knit approx. 3 sts for every 4 rows along the curved edge of Right front, working from side edge to shoulder. Work 8 rows in Twisted Rib. BO loosely in rib. Sew Right front onto the right side of the Back aligning at the armhole. Join front and back shoulders using 3-needle BO. Leave rem back neck sts on holder.

Pattern repeat

Knit
RS: knit
WS: purl

Purl
RS: purl
WS: knit

Small Chevron Pattern

Large Chevron Pattern

Medium Chevron Pattern

Using smaller needle and 2 strands of CC, with RS facing pick up and knit approx. 2 sts for every 3 rows along the curved edge of Center front, working from neck edge to side. Work 8 rows in Twisted Rib. BO loosely in rib. Sew Center front to right side of Back, below Right front, so that ribbed bands of Right front and Center front overlap with Center front band on top.

Using smaller needle and 2 strands of CC, pick up and knit approx. 3 sts for every 4 rows along straight edge of Center front and work 8 rows in Twisted Rib. BO loosely in rib. Repeat along straight edge of Left front.

Using smaller needle and 2 strands of CC, knit up the back neck sts and work 8 rows Twisted Rib. BO loosely in rib. Seam edges of neck ribbing to edges of Right front and Left front ribbings.

Using dpn and 2 strands of CC, pick up and knit 1 st in every st and 3 sts in every 4 rows around armhole, beg at center underarm and ending with an even number of sts. Work 8 rnds Twisted Rib. BO loosely in rib. Rep for second armhole.

Weave in all ends. Soak in warm water, lay flat to dry. Once dry, place buttons where desired referencing photos, sew in place through both layers.

[13, 13.25, 14][14.75, 15, 15.75, 16][16.75, 17.25, 17.75]in
[33, 33.5, 35.5][37.5, 38, 40, 40.5][42.5, 44, 45]cm

[2, 2.25, 2.5][2.75, 2.75, 3, 3.25][3.25, 3.75, 3.75]in
[5, 5.5, 6.5][7, 7, 7.5, 8.5][8.5, 9.5, 9.5]cm

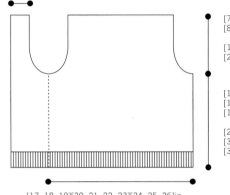

[7, 7.25, 7.5][7.75, 8, 8.25, 8.5]
[8.75, 9, 9.25]in

[18, 18.5, 19][19.5, 20, 20.5, 21]
[22, 23, 23.5]cm

[11.25, 11.5, 11.75]
[12, 12.25, 12.5, 12.75]
[13, 13.25, 13.5]in

[27.5, 28, 30]
[30.5, 31, 32, 32.5]
[33, 33.5, 34.5]cm

[17, 18, 19][20, 21, 22, 23][24, 25, 26]in
[43, 45.5, 48.5][51, 53.5, 56, 58.5][61, 63.5, 66]cm

[4, 4.5, 5][5.25, 5.75, 6.25, 6.75][7, 7.5, 7.75]in
[10, 11, 12.5][13.5, 14.5, 15.5, 17][18, 19, 19.5]cm

[7, 7, 7][7.25, 7.25, 7.75, 7.75][8, 8, 8.25]in
[18, 18, 18][18.5, 18.5, 19.5, 19.5][20.5, 20.5, 21]cm

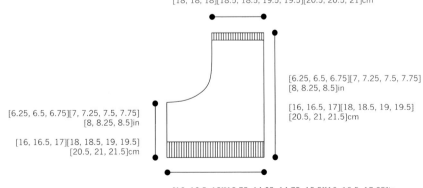

[6.25, 6.5, 6.75][7, 7.25, 7.5, 7.75]
[8, 8.25, 8.5]in

[16, 16.5, 17][18, 18.5, 19, 19.5]
[20.5, 21, 21.5]cm

[6.25, 6.5, 6.75][7, 7.25, 7.5, 7.75]
[8, 8.25, 8.5]in

[16, 16.5, 17][18, 18.5, 19, 19.5]
[20.5, 21, 21.5]cm

[12, 12.5, 13][13.75, 14.25, 14.75, 15.5][16, 16.5, 17.25]in
[30.5, 31.5, 33][35, 36, 37.5, 39.5][40.5, 42, 44]cm

[7, 7.25, 7.5][7.75, 8, 8.25, 8.5]
[8.75, 9, 9.25]in

[18, 18.5, 19][19.5, 20, 20.5, 21]
[22, 23, 23.5]cm

4in/10cm

[4, 4.5, 5][5.25, 5.75, 6.25, 6.75][7, 7.5, 7.75]in
[10, 11, 12.5][13.5, 14.5, 15.5, 17][18, 19, 19.5]cm

chapter three

DIMENSIONAL FOLDS

CONCERTINA DRESS
コンチェルティーナドレス

This distinct A-lined dress will fit into any wardrobe, with its flattering shape as well as intricate detailing around the neckline. Linen's flowing drape will keep you cool on hot summer days, perfect for layering over a pair of leggings or jeans. For cooler evening occasions throw on a classic jacket for a more elegant look.

by VANESSA YAP-EINBUND

SIZES

To fit bust size [32, 34, 36][38, 40, 42, 44][46, 48, 50]in/
[81, 86.5, 91.5][96.5, 101.5, 106.5, 112][117, 122, 127]cm

Finished measurements [32, 34, 36][38, 40, 42, 44][46, 48, 50]
in/[81, 86.5, 91.5][96.5, 101.5, 106.5, 112][117, 122, 127]cm

Length [30.5, 31.25, 31.75][32.5, 33, 33.25, 33.75][34.25,
34.75, 35.25]in/[77.5, 79.25, 80.5][82.5, 83.75, 84.5, 85.5]
[87, 88.25, 89.5]cm

YARN

Habu Textiles XS-21 20/2 linen, 100% linen; 218yds(199m)/
oz(28g); 2 (natural)
[12, 12.5, 13.5][14, 15, 15.5, 16.5][17, 18, 18.5]oz/[330, 350,
371][392, 412, 433, 453][474, 495, 515]g
OR
[2565, 2725, 2886][3046, 3206, 3367, 3527][3687, 3848, 4008]
yds/[2342, 2488, 2635][2781, 2928, 3074, 3220][3367, 3513,
3659]m
Worked with 2 strands held together

NEEDLES

4 mm 24in circular
3 mm 24in circular (or size to obtain gauge)

NOTIONS

Stitch markers
Stitch holders
Crochet hook
Scrap yarn
Tapestry needle
Sewing needle and matching thread

GAUGE

22 sts and 24 rows in 4in/10cm over washed and blocked St st
swatch worked in a round on larger needle with 2 strands held
together

NOTES

Please pay attention as linen grows significantly in length and
produces stretchy knit fabric. Due to this factor take time to
check your gauge. For best fit knit with zero or negative ease.

BODY
Hem

Using Provisional method with scrap yarn and crochet hook CO
[220, 230, 242][252, 264, 274, 286][296, 308, 318] sts onto
smaller needle. Join in a round carefully not to twist. Pm at the
join. Change to Main yarn.

K [110, 115, 121][126, 132, 137, 143][148, 154, 159], pm, k
[110, 115, 121][126, 132, 137, 143][148, 154, 159] sts.
K 2 rnds, p 1 rnd, k 3 rnds.

Remove scrap yarn from CO, transfer those sts to a spare
circular needle, fold work along p rnd with WS tog and k1 st
from current rnd with 1 st from CO rnd to end. Switch to bigger
needle. Work [5, 0, 0][0, 3, 3, 4][5, 0, 1] rnds straight.

HIP SHAPING

Work straight for [11, 12, 12][12, 12, 12, 12][12, 13, 13] rnds.
Dec rnd: * Slm, k2tog, work to 2 sts before next m, ssk, slm,
k2tog, work to 2 sts before next m, ssk*.
Repeat previous [12, 13, 13][13, 13, 13, 13][13, 14, 14] rnds
total of 11 times.

Work [5, 1, 3][5, 3, 4, 5][5, 0, 1] rnds straight.
[176, 186, 198][208, 220, 230, 242][252, 264, 274] sts rem.
Place [88, 93, 99][104, 110, 115, 121][126, 132, 137] sts for
the front on a stitch holder. From this point dress is worked flat.

BACK

BO [3, 3, 3][3, 4, 4, 4][4, 5, 5] sts in the beg of the next 2 rows.
BO [2, 1, 2][2, 2, 2, 3][3, 3, 3] sts in the beg of the foll 2 rows.
Continue dec 1 st in the beg and end of every RS row total of
[6, 8, 9][10, 11, 12, 12][13, 14, 15] times in the foll manner:
Row 1 (RS): K1, ssk, work to last 3 sts, k2tog, k1.
Row 2 and all (WS) rows: P.

Work straight till armhole measures [6.25, 6.5, 6.75][7, 7.25,
7.5, 7.75][8, 8.25, 8.5]in/[16, 16.5, 17][18, 18.5, 19, 19.5]
[20.5, 21, 21.5]cm and start back neckline shaping.

Next row (RS): K [15, 15, 16][16, 17, 18, 18][19, 20, 21], BO
[36, 39, 39][42, 42, 43, 47][48, 48, 49], k [15, 15, 16][16, 17,
18, 18][19, 20, 21] sts.

Left shoulder

WS row: P to last 3 sts, p2tog tbl, p1.
RS row: K 1, ssk, k to end.
Next row: P to last 3 sts, p2tog tbl, p1. Place all sts on stitch
holder.

Right shoulder
Rejoin yarn on WS.
WS row: P1, p2tog, p to end.
RS row: K to last 3 sts, k2tog, k1.
Next row: P1, p2tog, p to end.
Place all sts on stitch holder.

FRONT
Transfer front sts from stitch holder onto needle. Rejoin yarn on RS and immediately start armhole shaping.
BO [3, 3, 3][3, 4, 4, 4][4, 5, 5] sts in the beg of the next 2 rows.
BO [2, 1, 2][2, 2, 2, 3][3, 3, 3] sts in the beg of the foll 2 rows.
Continue dec 1 st in the beg and end of every RS row total of [6, 8, 9][10, 11, 12, 12][13, 14, 15] times in the foll manner:
Row 1 (RS): K1, ssk, work to last 3 sts, k2tog, k1.
Row 2 and all (WS) rows: P.

AT THE SAME TIME
when armhole measures 2in/5cm start front neckline shaping.

Next row (RS): K [17, 17, 18][18, 19, 20, 20][21, 22, 23], BO [32, 35, 35][38, 38, 39, 43][44, 44, 45], k [17, 17, 18][18, 19, 20, 20][21, 22, 23] sts.

Right shoulder
Next row: P.
Next row: K 1, ssk, k to end.
Repeat previous 2 rows total of 5 times and then continue working straight till armhole measures [6.75, 7, 7.25][7.5, 7.75, 8, 8.25][8.5, 8.75, 9]in/[17, 18, 18.5][19, 19.5, 20.5, 21][21.5, 22, 23]cm.

Place all sts on needle holder.

Left shoulder
Rejoin yarn on WS.
Next row: P.
Next row: K to last 3 sts, k2tog, k1.
Repeat previous 2 rows total of 5 times and then continue working straight till armhole measures [6.75, 7, 7.25][7.5, 7.75, 8, 8.25][8.5, 8.75, 9]in/[17, 18, 18.5][19, 19.5, 20.5, 21][21.5, 22, 23]cm.

Place all sts on needle holder.

CONCERTINA NECKLINE TREATMENT

Make 2 strips.
Using smaller needle and 2 strands of Main yarn CO 14 sts.
Start working in foll patt: Sl,*p1, k1*, p1.
Then follow instructions below:
Rows 1-12: Work in patt.
Row 13: K.
Rows 14-24: Work in patt.
Row 25: K.
Repeat previous 25 rows total of [12, 12, 12][13, 13, 13, 14]
[14, 14, 15] times.

FINISHING

Using Grafting (Kitchener stitch) and darning needle join front and back shoulders together. Weave in all ends. Soak dress and the strips in warm water. Lay flat to dry. Linen takes particularly long to dry, turn dress over couple times. Fold each strip at the creases and press down with hot iron through cloth. Apply starch if desired. If you press with steam let the strips completely dry before proceeding.

Start by pinning down 2 strips on end forming "L" figure. Fold the left strip over the right one foll the schematics. Repeat to the end of the strips. Sew beg and end of the folding strips to prevent concertina from unraveling. Hold both ends and pin to right shoulder seam and sew in place on the neckline. Untwist concertina gently to reach necessary length to go around front neckline to left shoulder seam. Sew in place. It's best to secure concertina by sewing it in several spots along the neckline.

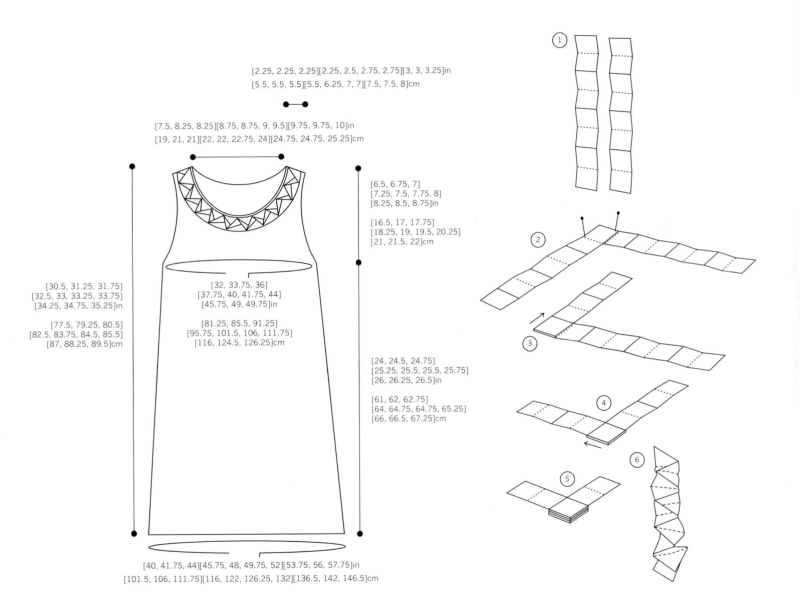

[2.25, 2.25, 2.25][2.25, 2.5, 2.75, 2.75][3, 3, 3.25]in
[5.5, 5.5, 5.5][5.5, 6.25, 7, 7][7.5, 7.5, 8]cm

[7.5, 8.25, 8.25][8.75, 8.75, 9, 9.5][9.75, 9.75, 10]in
[19, 21, 21][22, 22, 22.75, 24][24.75, 24.75, 25.25]cm

[6.5, 6.75, 7]
[7.25, 7.5, 7.75, 8]
[8.25, 8.5, 8.75]in

[16.5, 17, 17.75]
[18.25, 19, 19.5, 20.25]
[21, 21.5, 22]cm

[30.5, 31.25, 31.75]
[32.5, 33, 33.25, 33.75]
[34.25, 34.75, 35.25]in

[77.5, 79.25, 80.5]
[82.5, 83.75, 84.5, 85.5]
[87, 88.25, 89.5]cm

[32, 33.75, 36]
[37.75, 40, 41.75, 44]
[45.75, 49, 49.75]in

[81.25, 85.5, 91.25]
[95.75, 101.5, 106, 111.75]
[116, 124.5, 126.25]cm

[24, 24.5, 24.75]
[25.25, 25.5, 25.5, 25.75]
[26, 26.25, 26.5]in

[61, 62, 62.75]
[64, 64.75, 64.75, 65.25]
[66, 66.5, 67.25]cm

[40, 41.75, 44][45.75, 48, 49.75, 52][53.75, 56, 57.75]in
[101.5, 106, 111.75][116, 122, 126.25, 132][136.5, 142, 146.5]cm

AIRFOIL SKIRT
翼スカート

Have you ever thought a skirt could be versatile? This garment has knit-in side flaps, no seams and is reversible! Thanks to this construction it can be transformed into multiple ways. Overlap flaps in the front, tie them or close with a snap. Invert them on the sides to get deep pockets or fold them to the front to get a pencil skirt look. The unique yarn combination provides enough body to avoid transparency in the finished fabric and yet creates a flattering fit with elasticity.

by OLGA BURAYA-KEFELIAN

SIZES

To fit hip size [34, 36, 38][40, 42, 44, 46][48, 50, 52]in/[86, 91.5, 96.5][101.5, 106.5, 112, 117][122, 127, 132]cm

Length [23.75, 24, 24.25][24.5, 24.75, 25, 25.25][25.5, 25.75, 26]in/[60.5, 61, 61.5][62, 63, 63.5, 64][65, 65.5, 66]cm

YARN

Habu Textiles A-1 2/17 tsumugi silk, 100% silk; 265yds(239m)/oz(28g); 53 (cork)
[3.5, 3.5, 4][4, 4.5, 4.5, 5][5, 5.5, 5.5]oz/[93, 98, 104][110, 115, 120, 126][131, 137, 142]g
OR
[877, 928, 980][1032, 1083, 1135, 1186][1238, 1289, 1341] yds/[794, 837, 887][930, 977, 1023, 1070][1116, 1163, 1210]m

Habu Textiles A-62 1/10 paper moire, 50% linen, 50% cotton; 311yds(280m)/oz(28g); 3 (wine)
[3, 3, 3.5][3.5, 4, 4, 4][4.5, 4.5, 4.5]oz/[79, 84, 89][94, 99, 103, 108][113, 117, 122]g
OR
[882, 933, 985][1037, 1089, 1141, 1193][1244, 1296, 1348] yds/[794, 840, 887][934, 981, 1028, 1075][1120, 1167, 1214]m

NEEDLES

3.75 mm 24in, 36in, 47in, 60in circular (or size to obtain gauge)

NOTIONS

6 stitch markers (3 colors)
2 row counters
1·2yds 1in wide elastic ribbon
1 x .5in clothing snap (optional)
Tapestry needle

GAUGE

20 sts and 32 rounds in 4in/10cm over washed and blocked St st swatch knit in a round with both yarns held together

NOTES

The skirt is worked in a round with 2 yarns throughout. Keep switching to longer circular needle when current needle becomes too crowded with stitches.

BODY

Using Cable method and shortest needle CO [150, 160, 170][180, 190, 200, 210][220, 230, 240] sts. Join in a round, pm (1st color), k [75, 80, 85][90, 95, 100, 105][110, 115, 120] sts, pm (2nd color), k [75, 80, 85][90, 95, 100, 105][110, 115, 120] sts. Continue working in St st for 4in/10cm from CO edge. Then work [10, 15, 13][13, 10, 9, 17][16, 15, 14] rnds straight.

Side flap increases

(pm in 3rd color)
Setup rnd: *Slm, kfb, kfb, pm, k to 2 sts before next m, pm, kfb, kfb, slm, kfb, kfb, pm, k to 2 sts before next m, pm, kfb, kfb.*

Work [5, 4, 4][4, 4, 4, 3][3, 3, 3] rnds straight.
Increase rnd: *Slm, kfb, k to 1 st before m, kfb, slm, k to next m, slm, kfb, k to 1 st before m, kfb, slm, kfb, k to 1 st before m, kfb, slm, k to next m, slm, kfb, k to 1 st before m, kfb.*
Repeat those previous [6, 5, 5][5, 5, 5, 4][4, 4, 4] rnds total of [19, 21, 22][23, 24, 25, 27][28, 29, 30] times.
Work [6, 18, 15][12, 9, 6, 26][24, 22, 20] rnds straight.

Hip increase

AT THE SAME TIME (introduce second row counter)
When skirt measures 4in/10cm from CO edge start Hip increases.
Work [9, 9, 9][10, 10, 10, 10][11, 11, 11, 11] rnds straight.
Hip increase rnd: *Slm, follow instructions for your side flap work to second m, slm, kfb, work to 1 st before next m, kfb, slm, follow instructions for side flap, slm, follow instructions for side flap, slm, kfb, work to 1 st before next m, kfb, slm, follow instructions for side flap*.
Repeat previous [10, 10, 10][11, 11, 11, 11][12, 12, 12] rnds total of 9 times.
Work [4, 6, 8][1, 3, 5,7][0, 2, 4] rnds straight.

Hip decrease

Work 15 rnds straight.
Hip decrease rnd: *Slm, follow instructions for your side flap work to second m, slm, ssk, work to 2 st before next m, k2tog, slm, follow instructions for side flap, slm, follow instructions for side flap, slm, ssk, work to 2 st before next m, k2tog, slm, follow instructions for side flap*.
Repeat previous 16 rnds once again.

At this point all your side flap increases should be complete. [338, 364, 382][400, 418, 436, 462][480, 498, 516] sts total on the needle.

Fold the side flaps at the middle marker and perform a 3-needle BO (or Kitchener stitch) on the inside of the skirt all the way to the hip markers. Transfer remaining [170,180, 190][200, 210, 220, 230][240, 250, 260] sts onto smallest circular needle, re-distribute markers to indicate side seams.
Work 4 rnds straight.
Continue high hip decrease.

Decr rnd: *Slm, ssk, k to 2 sts before next m, k2tog, slm, ssk, k to 2 sts before next m, k2tog*.
Work 1 rnds straight.

Repeat previous 2 rnds total of 10 times. [130, 140, 150][160, 170, 180, 190][200, 210, 220] sts.

Waistband casing
Work straight for 8 rnds.
P next rnd.
Work 8 rnds straight. Do not BO.
Measure elastic around your waist, cut overlapping by 1in/2.5cm. Sew elastic together to form a round.
Fold casing in half at the purl rnd, insert elastic into the casing, align and pin evenly on the inside, whip stitch live sts onto the body of the skirt with Main yarn.

FINISHING
Soak the skirt. Block lightly. Try on the skirt, holding the tips of each side flaps fold to the front, tug on them and overlap a little to mark placement for a snap. Sew the snap on.

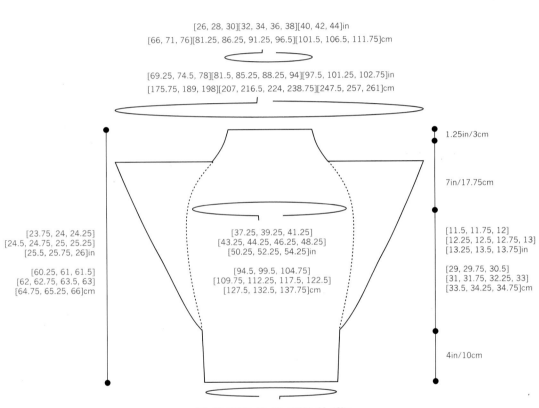

[26, 28, 30][32, 34, 36, 38][40, 42, 44]in
[66, 71, 76][81.25, 86.25, 91.25, 96.5][101.5, 106.5, 111.75]cm

[69.25, 74.5, 78][81.5, 85.25, 88.25, 94][97.5, 101.25, 102.75]in
[175.75, 189, 198][207, 216.5, 224, 238.75][247.5, 257, 261]cm

1.25in/3cm

7in/17.75cm

[23.75, 24, 24.25]
[24.5, 24.75, 25, 25.25]
[25.5, 25.75, 26]in

[60.25, 61, 61.5]
[62, 62.75, 63.5, 63]
[64.75, 65.25, 66]cm

[37.25, 39.25, 41.25]
[43.25, 44.25, 46.25, 48.25]
[50.25, 52.25, 54.25]in

[94.5, 99.5, 104.75]
[109.75, 112.25, 117.5, 122.5]
[127.5, 132.5, 137.75]cm

[11.5, 11.75, 12]
[12.25, 12.5, 12.75, 13]
[13.25, 13.5, 13.75]in

[29, 29.75, 30.5]
[31, 31.75, 32.25, 33]
[33.5, 34.25, 34.75]cm

4in/10cm

[30, 32, 34][36, 38, 40, 42][44, 46, 48]in
[76, 81.5, 86.25][91.25, 96.5, 101.5, 106.5][111.75, 116.75, 122]cm

FOLDOVER TOP
フォールドオーヴァートップ

The light fabric created for this garment has plenty of potential; silk wrapped stainless steel makes it incredibly malleable. If you wish to experiment with texture, roll the garment in a tight ball that will surprise you with crushed pleated texture once straightened. The minimalistic look combines simple, yet innovative construction that emphasizes the shoulders with minimal seaming. All edges are treated with various i-cord techniques to provide a refined look.

by OLGA BURAYA-KEFELIAN

SIZES

To fit bust size [32, 34, 36][38, 40, 42, 44][46, 48, 50]in/[81.5, 86.5, 91.5][96.5, 101.5, 106.5, 112][117, 122, 127]cm

Finished measurements [31.75, 33.75, 35.75][37.75, 39.75, 41.75, 43.75][45.75, 47.75, 49.75]in/[80.5, 85.75, 91][96, 101, 106, 111][116, 121.25, 126.25]cm

Length (hem to armhole) [13.75, 14, 14.25][14.5, 14.75, 15, 15.25][15.5, 15.75, 16]in/[34.5, 35.25, 36][36.75, 37.5, 38, 38.5][39.25, 39.75, 40.25]cm

YARN

Habu Textiles A-1 2/17 tsumugi silk, 100% silk; 265yds(239m)/oz(28g); 70 (lavender)
[3, 3, 3.5][3.5, 3.5, 4, 4][4, 4.5, 4.5]oz/[76, 81, 85][90, 95, 100, 104][109, 114, 119]g
OR
[707, 751, 795][840, 884, 928, 972][1016, 1060, 1105]yds/[638, 678, 717][757, 797, 837, 877][917, 956, 996]m

Habu Textiles A-20 silk wrapped stainless steel, 69% silk, 31% stainless steel; 622yds(566m)/oz(28g); 16 (lavender)
[1.5, 1.5, 1.5][2, 2, 2, 2][2, 2, 2.5]oz/[38, 40, 42][45, 47, 49, 52][54, 56, 59]g
OR
[830, 882, 933][985, 1037, 1089, 1141][1193, 1244, 1296]yds/[755, 802, 849][897, 944, 991, 1038][1085, 1132, 1180]m

NEEDLES

3.25 mm 24in circular
3.25 mm dpns, set of 5 (or size to obtain gauge)

NOTIONS

Stitch markers
Stitch holder
Scrap yarn
Crochet hook
Tapestry needle

GAUGE

28 sts and 36 rows in 4in/10cm in washed and blocked St st swatch knit in the round with both yarns held together

NOTES

Fabric created with these fibers is very stretchy and malleable. For best fit knit with zero or negative ease.

BODY

Using Provisional method with scrap yarn and crochet hook CO [230, 244, 258][272, 286, 300, 314][328, 342, 356] sts onto circular needle.

Switch to Main yarn and knit a row. At the end of the row join to work in a rnd, pm at the join. Then pm after [115, 122, 129][136, 143, 150, 157][164, 171, 178] sts from the first m. K 3 rnds total, p next rnd, then k 3 rnds.

Remove scrap yarn from CO, transfer those sts to a spare circular needle, fold work along p rnd with WS tog and k1 st from current rnd with 1 st from CO rnd to end.

Hip decreases
Work [5, 5, 5][5, 5, 5, 6][6, 6, 6] rnds straight.
Dec rnd: *Slm, k1, ssk, k to 3 sts before next m, k2tog, k1, slm, k1, ssk, k to 3 sts before next m, k2tog*.

Repeat previous [6, 6, 6][6, 6, 6, 7][7, 7, 7] rnds total of 7 times.
Then work [1, 3, 3][3, 5, 5, 0][0, 2, 2] rnds straight.

Bust increases
Work [14, 14, 15][15, 15, 16, 16][16, 16, 17] rnds straight.
Inc rnd: *Slm, k1, m1, k to 1 st before next m, m1, k1, slm, k1, m1, k to 1 st before next m, m1, k1.*
Repeat previous [15, 15, 16][16, 16, 17, 17][17, 17, 18] rnds total of 5 times.

Then work [3, 3, 1][3, 3, 0, 0][2, 2, 0] rnds straight. [222, 236, 250][264, 278, 292, 306][320, 334, 348] sts.
Place [111, 118, 125][132, 129, 146, 153][160, 167, 174] sts on a stitch holder for the back.
From this point top is worked flat.

UPPER FRONT
Armhole shaping
BO [5, 5, 5][6, 6, 6, 7][7, 8, 9] sts in the beg of next 2 rows.
BO [2, 3, 3][3, 4, 4, 4][4, 4, 5] sts in the beg of foll 2 rows.
Then continue to dec 1 st on side end total of [10, 11, 12][13, 14, 15, 17][18, 19, 20] times in the foll manner:
Row 1 (RS): Sl3 kwise, ssk, work to last 2 sts, k2tog, k3.
Row 2 (WS): Sl3 pwise, p to end.

Continue working straight slipping first 3 sts of each row until front measures [4.75, 4.75, 5][5, 5.25, 5.25, 5.5][5.5, 5.75, 5.75]in/[12, 12, 12.5][12.5, 13.5, 13.5, 14][14, 14.5, 14.5]cm from armhole.
End on WS.

Applied I-cord
Sl first 3 sts onto a dpn, slide those sts to beg of a needle and with second dpn k3.
Slide sts again.
* K1, kfb, sl next st, k 1 sts from the front edge, psso.* Slide 4 sts to beg of the needle.

Repeat previous row until 3 sts of the front rem. K1, k2tog, k1.
Graft (Kitchener stitch) 3 sts from dpn together with 3 rem sts of the body.

UPPER BACK
Rejoin yarn on RS.
Sl 3 sts in the beg of each row and continue working in St st until back measures [7.5, 7.75, 8][8.25, 8.5, 8.75, 9][9.25, 9.5, 9.75]in/[19, 19.5, 20.5][21, 21.5, 22, 23][23.5, 24, 25]cm from armhole. End with WS row.

Transfer center [35, 38, 39][38, 39, 40, 43][44, 43, 44] sts on a stitch holder.

SHOULDER AND NECKLINE SHAPING
Right side neckline
Dec 1 st on the neckline edge total of [22, 23, 24][25, 25, 26, 27][28, 30, 31] times in the foll manner:
Row 1 (RS): Work in patt to last 3 sts, k2tog, k1.
Row 2 (WS): Work in patt.

AT THE SAME TIME
Work on Right shoulder.
[38, 40, 43][47, 50, 53, 55][58, 62, 65] sts.
Work [2, 2, 2][1, 1, 1, 1][1, 1, 1] rows straight.
Dec row (RS): Sl3 kwise, ssk, work to end in patt.
Continue working in St st always slipping first 3 sts on armhole edge.

Repeat dec row on every [3, 3, 3]rd[2, 2, 2, 2][2, 2, 2]nd row total of [13, 14, 16][19, 22, 24, 25][27, 30, 31] times.
(If dec row is on WS: P to 5 sts to end, p2tog tbl, p3.)
Total of [13, 14, 16][19, 22, 24, 25][27, 30, 31] sts decreased within [44, 46, 48][50, 50, 52, 54][56, 60, 62] rows.
Transfer rem 3 sts on a stitch holder.

Left side neckline
Rejoin yarn at the left shoulder on RS and immediately start neckline shaping.
Dec 1 st on the neckline edge total of [22, 23, 24][25, 25, 26, 27][28, 30, 31] times in the foll manner:
Row 1 (RS): K1, ssk, work to end in patt.
Row 2 (WS): Sl3 kwise, work in patt.

AT THE SAME TIME
Work on Left shoulder
[38, 40, 43][47, 50, 53, 55][58, 62, 65] sts.
Work [2, 2, 2][1, 1, 1, 1][1, 1, 1] rows straight.
Dec row (RS): Work to last 5 sts, k2tog, k3.
Continue working in St st always slipping first 3 sts on armhole edge.

Repeat dec row on every [3, 3, 3]rd[2, 2, 2, 2][2, 2, 2]nd row total of [13, 14, 16][19, 22, 24, 25][27, 30, 31] times.
(If dec row is on WS: Sl3 pwise, p2tog, p to end in patt.)
Total of [13, 14, 16][19, 22, 24, 25][27, 30, 31] sts decreased within [44, 46, 48][50, 50, 52, 54][56, 60, 62] rows.
Transfer rem 3 sts on a stitch holder.

FINISHING
Transfer 3 sts from Right shoulder onto a double pointed needle. Rejoin yarn.
Work applied I-cord (see above) around entire right neckline edge, over back neckline and left neckline edge. Graft (Kitchener stitch) 3 sts of Left shoulder onto 3 live sts from the dpn.

Measure [2, 2.25, 2.5][2.75, 2.75, 3, 3.25][3.5, 3.75, 4]in/[5, 5.5, 6.5][7, 7, 7.5, 8.5][9, 9.5, 10]cm of the outer armhole edge on each side of the top, fold it over towards the front and mattress stitch it to [2, 2.25, 2.5][2.75, 2.75, 3, 3.25][3.5, 3.75, 4]in/[5, 5.5, 6.5][7, 7, 7.5, 8.5][9, 9.5, 10]cm of the front on each side (see schematic).

Belt
Using Main yarn and dpn CO 5 sts. Slide needle to the beg of the row and k 5. Continue working on I-cord till it measures [41, 43, 45][47, 49, 51, 53][55, 57, 59]in/[104, 109, 114.5][119.5, 124.5, 129.5, 134.5][139.5, 145, 150]cm. BO all sts.

Lightly soak in warm water and block. Due to nature of silk stainless steel yarn in the fabric, the garment will move and drape as desired.

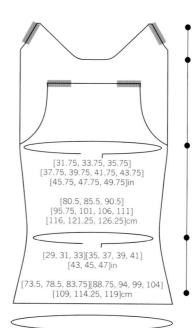

[4.75, 5, 5.25][5.5, 5.5, 5.75, 6]
[6.25, 6.5, 7]in

[12, 12.5, 13.25][14, 14, 14.5, 15]
[15.75, 16.5, 17.75]cm

[7.5, 7.75, 8][8.25, 8.5, 8.75, 9]
[9.25, 9.5, 9.75]in

[19, 19.5, 20.25][21, 21.5, 22, 22.75]
[23.5, 24, 24.75]cm

[31.75, 33.75, 35.75]
[37.75, 39.75, 41.75, 43.75]
[45.75, 47.75, 49.75]in

[80.5, 85.5, 90.5]
[95.75, 101, 106, 111]
[116, 121.25, 126.25]cm

[8.75, 8.75, 9][9.25, 9.25, 9.5, 9.5]
[9.75, 9.75, 10]in

[22, 22, 22.75][23.5, 23.5, 24, 24]
[24.75, 24.75, 25.25]cm

[29, 31, 33][35, 37, 39, 41]
[43, 45, 47]in

[73.5, 78.5, 83.75][88.75, 94, 99, 104]
[109, 114.25, 119]cm

[5, 5.25, 5.25][5.25, 5.5, 5.5, 5.75]
[5.75, 6, 6]in

[12.5, 13.25, 13.25][13.25, 14, 14, 14.5]
[14.5, 15, 15]cm

[33, 35, 37][39, 41, 43, 45][47, 49, 51]in

[83.75, 88.75, 94][99, 104, 109, 114.25]
[119.25, 124.5, 129.5]cm

chapter four

NAUTICAL STRUCTURES

CORALLIUM SCARF
珊瑚色のスカーフ

As a fiber, bamboo has incredible features of drape and
silkiness, which develops into a wonderfully soft and
supple fabric. This design disguises and capitalizes
on the natural growth that occurs with bamboo yarn,
often seen as a negative feature of this wonderful plant
fiber. Textured stitches and peaks are enhanced with the
yarn's vibrant color. This scarf provides a complemen-
tary accessory for any outfit, or season, while caressing
your neck.

by OLGA BURAYA-KEFELIAN

SIZE
Length 68in/172.5cm
Width 7in/18cm

YARN
Habu Textiles XS-32 20/18 bamboo, 100% bamboo;
57.5yds(52m)/oz(28g); 5 (red)
9oz/252g
OR
518yds/468m

NEEDLE
3.5 mm (or size to obtain gauge)

NOTIONS
Stitch holders
Tapestry needle

GAUGE
24 sts and 28 rows in 4in/10cm over washed and blocked garter
stitch swatch

NOTES
The scarf consists of pattern Repeat 1, pattern Repeat 2 and
garter stitch sections. Weave in ends as you join each sequence
into garter stitch section.

SCARF

Using your favorite method CO 42 sts. Work 7 rows in garter st. From this point on you are going to work on 6 sts at a time that are called sequences.

Repeat 1

First, third, fifth, and seventh 6-st sequences are worked in garter st as foll:
RS: K.
WS: K.
Work a total of 18 rows, cut yarn (leaving a 4in/10cm tail) and place sts on a holder.

Rejoin yarn.
Second, fourth, and sixth 6-st sequences are worked in St st with a garter st border as foll:
RS: Knit.
WS: K1, p4, k1.
Work a total of 18 rows, cut yarn (leaving a 4in/10cm tail) and place sts on another holder.
Do not cut the yarn after 7th sequence.

Garter section
Turn work.
WS: Knit across all sts, giving a half-twist to the left to the first, third, fifth, and seventh sequences before working across them.
Continue in garter st for a further 10 rows.

Repeat 2
First, third, fifth, and seventh 6-st sequences are worked in St st with a garter st border as foll:
RS: Knit.
WS: K1, p4, k1.
Work a total of 18 rows, cut yarn (leaving a 4in/10cm tail) and place sts on a holder.

Rejoin yarn.
Second, forth, sixth 6-st sequences are worked in garter st as foll:
RS: K.
WS: K.
Work a total of 18 rows, cut yarn (leaving a 4in/10cm tail) and place sts on another holder.
Do not cut the yarn after the 7th sequence.

Garter section
Turn work.
WS: Knit across all sts, giving a half-twist to the right to the second, fourth and sixth sequences before working across them.
Continue in garter st for a further 10 rows.*
Repeat from * to * a total of 15 times, then work Repeat 1 and

Garter section once more, ending with 6 rows only of garter st after joining. BO all sts.

FINISHING
Weave in all ends. Lightly soak in lukewarm water. Lay flat to dry. Bamboo is prone to growing, so unless you wish for your scarf to be longer do not hang to dry.

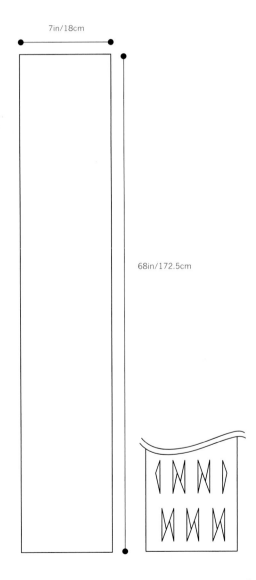

7in/18cm

68in/172.5cm

JAPONICA CRAVAT
椿ネクタイ

This wonderfully organic neckpiece utilizes malleable
stainless steel threads worked together in contrasting
colors to provide an intriguing color depth. Lighter than
air fabric can be manipulated to form fluttering tendrils
floating freely or flared for a more ruffled appearance or
scrunched for a modern crumpled style. Experiment and
enjoy the possibilities this design piece provides.

by KIRSTEN JOHNSTONE

SIZE
Length 61in/155cm

YARN
Habu Textiles A-20/21 silk wrapped stainless steel; 69% silk, 31% stainless steel; 622yds(566m)/oz(28g); 3 (gray)
1 oz/28 gr OR 622 yds/566m

Habu Textiles A-20/21 silk wrapped stainless steel; 69% silk, 31% stainless steel; 622yds(566m)/oz(28g); 21 (violet)
1 oz/28 gr OR 622 yds/566m

NEEDLES
3.25 mm 24in or dpns, set of 5
3.75 mm (or size to obtain gauge)

NOTIONS
Stitch holders
Tapestry needle

GAUGE
30 sts and 34 rows in 4in/10cm in St st with both yarns held together on smaller needle

23 sts and 32 rows in 4in/10cm in St st with both yarns held together on larger needle

NOTES
Cravat is worked in 3 pieces. 2 ruffles are knit separate, then attached while knitting cravat piece.

 RUFFLES
Right ruffle
Using a strand of each yarn and larger needle, CO 120 sts.
Work 2 rows in St st (k 1 row, p 1 row).
Next Row (RS): K.
Dec Row (WS): P to last 3 sts, p2tog, p1.
Rep previous 2 rows 4 times total.

Continue decreasing and AT THE SAME TIME start Short row shaping:
Next Row (RS): K to last 10 sts, sl next st, w&t.
Dec Row (WS): P to last 3 sts, p2tog, p1.

Next Row: K to 10 sts before last wrap, sl next st, w&t.
Dec Row: P to last 3 sts, p2tog, p1.
Rep previous 2 rows 4 times total.

Next Row (RS): K to 5 sts before last wrap, sl next st, w&t.
Next Row (WS): P to last 3 sts, p2tog, p1.
Rep previous 2 rows 8 times total.

Next Row (RS): K to 5 sts before last wrap, sl next st, w&t.
Next Row (WS): P to end.
Next Row (RS): K across all sts, picking up and knitting wraps together with wrapped sts.
103 sts.

Next Row (WS): *P3tog*, rep from * to * until 22 st rem, *p2tog*, rep from * to * to end of row.
38 sts.
Place ruffle on a stitch holder.

Left ruffle
Using a strand of each yarn and larger needle, CO 120 sts.
Work 2 rows in St st (k 1 row, p 1 row).
Next Row (RS): K to last 3 sts, k2tog, k1.
Next Row (WS): P.
Rep previous 2 rows 4 times total.

Continue decreasing and AT THE SAME TIME start Short row shaping:
Next Row (WS): P to last 10 sts, sl next st, w&t.
Dec Row (RS): K to last 3 sts, k2tog, k1.

Next Row (WS): P to 10 sts before last wrap, sl next st, w&t.
Dec Row (RS): K to last 3 sts, k2tog, k1.
Rep the last 2 rows 4 times total.

Next Row (WS): P to 5 sts before last wrap, sl next st, w&t.
Next Row (RS): K in patt till 3 sts rem, k2tog, k1.
Rep the last 2 rows 8 times total.

Next Row (WS): P to 5 sts before last wrap, sl next st, w&t.
Next Row (RS): Knit.
Next Row (WS): P across all sts, picking up and purling wraps together with wrapped sts.
103 sts.

Next Row (RS): *K3tog*, rep from * to * until 22 st rem, *k2tog*, rep * to * to end of row.
38 sts.
Place ruffle on a stitch holder.

CRAVAT
Right cravat tie
Using a strand of each yarn and smaller needle, CO 50 sts.
K 1 row, p 1 row.
Next Row (RS): K to 3 sts rem, k2tog, k1.
Work 3 rows straight in St st.
Rep previous 4 rows until 35 sts rem.

Next Row (RS): K to 3 sts rem, k2tog, k1.
Work 5 rows straight in St st.
Rep last 6 rows until 20 sts rem.

Work even in St st until work measures 19.5in/50cm from CO edge, ending on RS.
Next row: *K2tog*, rep from * to end of row.
10 sts rem. Do not break yarn.

Right ruffle attachment and I-cord
Next Row (RS): Slide all sts to other end of needle and k until 1 st rem, sl next st, transfer first of Right ruffle sts on RS (at large end of Ruffle) onto a needle and k it, psso.

Next Row (RS): Slide all sts to other end of needle and k until 1 st rem, sl next st, transfer next st on RS Right ruffle onto a needle and k it, psso.

Rep last row until all Right Ruffle sts have been incorporated. Continue working I-cord for another 9in/23cm.

Left ruffle attachment
Next Row (RS): Slide all sts to other end of needle and k until 1 st rem, sl next st, transfer first of Left ruffle sts on RS (at narrow end of Ruffle) onto a needle and k it, psso.

Next Row (RS): Slide all sts to other end of needle and k until 1 st rem, sl st, transfer next st on RS Left ruffle onto a needle and k it, psso.
Rep last row until all Left Ruffle sts have been incorporated.

Left cravat tie
Next Row (RS) (inc): *Kfb*, rep from * to * to end of row.
20 sts.
Next row (WS): P.

Next Row (RS) (inc): K to 2 sts rem, kfb, k1.
Work 5 rows straight in St st.
Rep previous 6 rows to 35 sts.
Next Row (RS): K to 2 sts rem, kfb, k1.
Work 3 rows straight in St st.
Rep previous 4 rows to 50 sts.

Work 2 rows St st.
BO all sts.

FINISHING
Soak in lukewarm water and lay flat to dry.

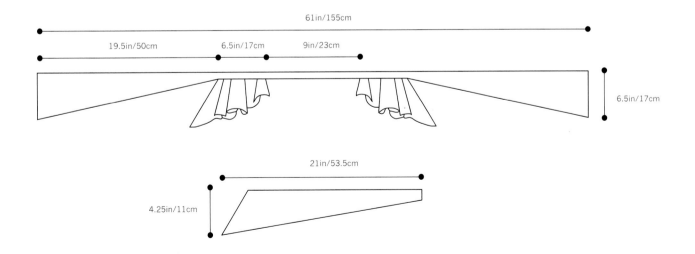

ABYSS JACKET
深海ジャケット

This jacket is a perfect addition to any wardrobe: with classic tailoring and minimalist feature details, this garment is a true crowd-pleaser. Cropped three-quarter sleeves compliment the feminine shaping and becomes an excellent candidate for layering with your favorite blouse. The amazing tsumugi silk color palette gives intense color saturation and at the same time adds dimensional texture. Experiment with color combinations to create a precise hue to suit your style.

by OLGA BURAYA-KEFELIAN

To fit bust size [32, 34, 36][38, 40, 42, 44][46, 48, 50]in/[81.5, 86.5, 91.5][96.5, 101.5, 106.5, 112][117, 122, 127]cm

Finished measurements [33.75, 36.25, 37.75][39.5, 42, 43.75, 45.5][48, 49.75, 51.75]in/[86, 92, 96][100.5, 106.5, 111, 115.5][122, 126.5, 131.5]cm

Length [22, 22.25, 22.5][23.75, 24, 24.5, 24.75][26.5, 26.75, 27]in/[56, 56.5, 57][60.5, 61, 62, 63][67.5, 68, 68.5]cm

YARN
Habu Textiles A-1 2/17 tsumugi silk, 100% silk; 265yds(239m)/oz(28g); 47 (dark blue)
[6, 6.5, 7][7.5, 8, 8, 8.5][9, 9, 9.5]oz/[168, 177, 190][200, 211, 221, 232][242, 253, 263]g
OR
[1590, 1690, 1789][1889, 1988, 2087, 2187][2286, 2386, 2485]yds/[1434, 1524, 1614][1703, 1793, 1883, 1972][2062, 2151, 2241]m
Worked with 2 strands held together

Habu Textiles A-1 2/17 tsumugi silk, 100% silk; 265yds(239m)/oz(28g); 50 (blue green)
[6, 6.5, 7][7.5, 8, 8, 8.5][9, 9, 9.5]oz/[168, 177, 190][200, 211, 221, 232][242, 253, 263]g
OR
[1590, 1690, 1789][1889, 1988, 2087, 2187][2286, 2386, 2485]yds/[1434, 1524, 1614][1703, 1793, 1883, 1972][2062, 2151, 2241]m
Worked with 2 strands held together

NEEDLES
5.5mm 24in circular
5.5mm dpns, set of 5 (or size to obtain gauge)

NOTIONS
Stitch markers
Stitch holders
Row counter
[10, 10, 10][11, 11, 11, 11][12, 12, 12] clothing snaps
Tapestry needle
Sewing needle
Matching sewing thread
2-3 yds grosgrain ribbon (optional)

GAUGE
19 sts and 25 rows in 4in/10cm over washed and blocked St st swatch knit with 4 strands held together

NOTES
This jacket is worked holding 4 strands together, 2 of each color. Body is knit in one piece until armhole, then back and fronts are worked flat. Sleeves are worked in a round until armhole, then sleeve caps are worked flat.

BODY

Using Cable method and circular needle CO [170, 182, 190][198, 210, 218, 226][238, 246, 256] sts.

Next row (WS): K [40, 43, 45][47, 50, 52, 54][57, 59, 62], pm, k [80, 86, 90][94, 100, 104, 108][114, 118, 124], pm, k [40, 43, 45][47, 50, 52, 54][57, 59, 62], pm, k 10.

Middle markers are to indicate each side and a marker to indicate a tab.

Continue working in Tab patt below.

Right Tab sequence

Row 1 (RS): K 10, k to end.

Row 2 (WS): K1, p to last m, p9, k1.

Work previous 2 rows total of 5 times.

On the 11th row BO first 10 sts in p, k to end, turn work, pm, using Cable method CO 10 sts.

Next continue working Left Tab sequence

Row 1 (WS): K1, p to last st, k1.

Row 2 (RS): K.

Work previous 2 rows total of 5 times.

On the 11th row BO first 10 sts in k, remove m, p to last st, k1, turn work, pm, using Cable method CO 10 sts.

Continue working Left and Right Tab sequences alternating them until body measures [13.5, 13.5, 13.5][14.5, 14.5, 14.5, 14.5][16, 16, 16]in/[34.5, 34.5, 34.5][37, 37, 37, 37][40.5, 40.5, 40.5]cm, end with WS.

From this point fronts and back are worked separate.

BACK

Worked on sts between Right and Left middle m(s).

Next row (RS): Work to Right armhole m, remove m, BO [3, 3, 3][3, 3, 3, 4][4, 5, 6] sts, work to next m, remove m, turn work, BO [3, 3, 3][3, 3, 3, 4][4, 5, 6] sts.

BO [2, 2, 2][2, 3, 3, 3][4, 4, 4] sts in the beg of foll 2 rows.

Dec row (RS): *Ssk, work to last 2 sts, k2tog*.

Next and all WS rows: P.

Repeat dec row on every RS row total of [5, 6, 7][8, 8, 9, 9][10, 10, 10] times. [60, 64, 66][68, 72, 74, 76][78, 80, 84] sts rem on the needle.

Work straight in patt until armhole measures [7.75, 8, 8.25][8.5, 8.75, 9, 9.25][9.5, 9.75, 10]in/[19.5, 20.5, 21][21.5, 22, 23, 23.5][24, 25, 25.5]cm. End with WS row.

Neckline and shoulder shaping

Next row (RS): K [22, 22, 23][23, 25, 25, 25][25, 26, 27] sts, sl 1, place next [14, 18, 18][20, 20, 22, 24][26, 26, 28] on one stitch holder and rem [23, 23, 24][24, 26, 26, 26][26, 27, 28] sts onto another stitch holder.

Right shoulder and neckline

RS: Slipped stitch · w&t.

Row 1 (WS): Beginnning at neckline, work in patt until [8, 8, 9][9, 10, 7, 7][7, 7, 7] sts from shoulder edge on left needle, sl next st, w&t.

Row 2 (RS): Work to [2, 2, 2][2, 2, 1, 1][1, 1, 1] sts before previous neckline wrap, sl next st, w&t.

Row 3: Work to [7, 7, 8][8, 9, 6, 6][6, 6, 7] sts before previous shoulder edge wrap, sl next st, w&t.

Row 4: Work to [2, 2, 2][2, 2, 1, 1][1, 1, 1] sts before previous neckline wrap, sl next st, w&t.

For bust sizes 32, 34, 36, 38, 40 only break yarn leaving 9in/23cm tail, place 19, 19, 20, 20, 22 shoulder sts and right back neckline sts on stitch holders.

Row 5: Work to [0, 0, 0][0, 0, 6, 6][6, 7, 7] sts before previous shoulder edge wrap, sl next st, w&t.

Row 6: Work to [0, 0, 0][0, 0, 1, 1][1, 1, 1] sts before previous neckline wrap, sl next st, w&t.

For bust sizes 42, 44, 46, 48, 50 only break yarn leaving 9in/23cm tail, place 23, 23, 23, 24, 25 shoulder sts and right back neckline sts on stitch holders.

Left shoulder and neckline

Transfer left shoulder sts from stitch holder onto needle. Rejoin yarn.

Row 1 (RS): Beginning at neckline edge, sl st (wrap yarn around it), work in patt until [8, 8, 9][9, 10, 7, 7][7, 7, 7] sts from shoulder edge left on left needle, sl next st, w&t.

Row 2 (WS): Work in patt until [2, 2, 2][2, 2, 1, 1][1, 1, 1] sts before previous neckline wrapped st, sl next st, w&t.

Row 3: Work to [7, 7, 8][8, 9, 6, 6][6, 6, 7] sts before previous shoulder edge wrap, sl next st, w&t.

Row 4: Work to [2, 2, 2][2, 2, 1, 1][1, 1, 1] sts before previous neckline wrap, sl next st, w&t.

For bust sizes 32, 34, 36, 38, 40 only break yarn leaving 9in/23cm tail, place 19, 19, 20, 20, 22 shoulder sts and left back neckline sts on stitch holders.

Row 5: Work to [0, 0, 0][0, 0, 6, 6][6, 7, 7] sts before previous shoulder edgewrap, sl next st, w&t.

Row 6: Work to [0, 0, 0][0, 0, 1, 1][1, 1, 1] sts before previous neckline wrap, sl next st, w&t.

For bust sizes 42, 44, 46, 48, 50 only break yarn leaving 9in/23cm tail, place 23, 23, 23, 24, 25 shoulder sts and left back neckline sts on stitch holders.

RIGHT FRONT

Armhole shaping

Rejoin yarn on WS at the armhole and immediately start armhole shaping while continuing Tab patt.

Row 1 (WS): BO [3, 3, 3][3, 3, 3, 4][4, 5, 6] sts, work to end.

Row 2 and all RS rows: Work in patt.

Row 3: BO [2, 2, 2][2, 3, 3, 3][4, 4, 4] sts, work to end.
Dec row (RS): *Work in patt to last 2 sts, k2tog*.
Repeat dec row on every RS row total of [5, 6, 7][8, 8, 9, 9][10, 10, 10] times.
Continue working straight in patt until armhole measures [5.5, 5.5, 5.5][6.5, 6.5, 6.5, 6.5][7, 7, 7]in/[14, 14, 14][16.5, 16.5, 16.5, 16.5][17.75, 17.75, 17.75]cm.

Right front neckline
Row 1 (WS): Work to [2, 2, 2][3, 3, 4, 5][4, 4, 5] sts before Tab marker (or edge depending what Tab patt you are working), sl next st, w&t.
Row 2 and all RS rows: Work in patt.
Row 3: Work to 2 sts from previous wrap, sl next st, w&t.
Repeat rows 2-3 total of [3, 4, 4][4, 4, 4, 4][5, 5, 5] times.

AT THE SAME TIME
Right front shoulder shaping
When armhole measures [7.75, 8, 8.25][8.5, 8.75, 9, 9.25][9.5, 9.75, 10]in/[19.5, 20.5, 21][21.5, 22, 23, 23.5][24, 25, 25.5]cm start shoulder shaping
Row 1 (RS): Beginning at neckline edge, sl st (wrap yarn around it), work in patt until [8, 8, 9][9, 10, 7, 7][7, 7, 7] sts from shoulder edge left on left needle, sl next st, w&t.
Row 2 (WS): Work in patt until [2, 2, 2][2, 2, 1, 1][1, 1, 1] sts before previous neckline wrapped st, sl next st, w&t.
Row 3: Work to [7, 7, 8][8, 9, 6, 6][6, 6, 7] sts before previous shoulder edge wrap, sl next st, w&t.
Row 4: Work to [2, 2, 2][2, 2, 1, 1][1, 1, 1] sts before previous neckline wrap, sl next st, w&t.
For bust sizes 32, 34, 36, 38, 40 only break yarn leaving 9in/23cm tail, place 19, 19, 20, 20, 22 shoulder sts and left back neckline sts on stitch holders.
Row 5: Work to [0, 0, 0][0, 0, 6, 6][6, 7, 7] sts before previous shoulder edge wrap, sl next st, w&t.
Row 6: Work to [0, 0, 0][0, 0, 1, 1][1, 1, 1] sts before previous neckline wrap, sl next st, w&t.
For bust sizes 42, 44, 46, 48, 50 only break yarn leaving 9in/23cm tail, place 23, 23, 23, 24, 25 shoulder sts and left back neckline sts on stitch holders.

LEFT FRONT
Armhole shaping
Rejoin yarn on RS at the armhole and immediately start armhole shaping while continuing Tab patt.
Row 1 (RS): BO [3, 3, 3][3, 3, 3, 4][4, 5, 6] sts, work to end.
Row 2 and all WS rows: Work in patt.
Row 3: BO [2, 2, 2][2, 3, 3, 3][4, 4, 4] sts, work to end.
Dec row (RS): *Ssk, work in patt to end*.
Repeat dec row on every RS row total of [5, 6, 7][8, 8, 9, 9][10, 10, 10] times.

Continue working straight in patt until armhole measures [5.5, 5.5, 5.5][6.5, 6.5, 6.5, 6.5][7, 7, 7]in/[14, 14, 14][16.5, 16.5, 16.5, 16.5][17.75, 17.75, 17.75]cm.

Left front neckline
Row 1 (RS): Work to [2, 2, 2][3, 3, 4, 5][4, 4, 5] sts before tab marker (or edge depending what Tab patt you are working), sl next st, w&t.
Row 2 and all WS rows: Work in patt.
Row 3: Work to 2 sts from previous wrap, sl next st, w&t.
Repeat rows 2-3 rows total of [3, 4, 4][4, 4, 4, 4][5, 5, 5] times.

AT THE SAME TIME

Left shoulder shaping
When armhole measures [7.75, 8, 8.25][8.5, 8.75, 9, 9.25][9.5, 9.75, 10]in/[19.5, 20.5, 21][21.5, 22, 23, 23.5][24, 25, 25.5]cm start shoulder shaping
Row 1 (WS): Beginnning at neckline, work in patt until [8, 8, 9][9, 10, 7, 7][7, 7, 7] sts from shoulder edge on left needle, sl next st, w&t.
Row 2 (RS): Work to [2, 2, 2][2, 2, 1, 1][1, 1, 1] sts before previous neckline wrap, sl next st, w&t.
Row 3: Work to [7, 7, 8][8, 9, 6, 6][6, 6, 7] sts before previous shoulder edge wrap, sl next st, w&t.
Row 4: Work to [2, 2, 2][2, 2, 1, 1][1, 1, 1] sts before previous neckline wrap, sl next st, w&t.
For bust sizes 32, 34, 36, 38, 40 only break yarn leaving 9in/23cm tail, place 19, 19, 20, 20, 22 shoulder sts and right back neckline sts on stitch holders.
Row 5: Work to [0, 0, 0][0, 0, 6, 6][6, 7, 7] sts before previous shoulder edge wrap, sl next st, w&t.
Row 6: Work to [0, 0, 0][0, 0, 1, 1][1, 1, 1] sts before previous neckline wrap, sl next st, w&t
For bust sizes 42, 44, 46, 48, 50 only break yarn leaving 9in/23cm tail, place 23, 23, 23, 24, 25 shoulder sts and right back neckline sts on stitch holders.

SLEEVES
(Make 2)
Using Cable method and dpns CO [58, 59, 61][64, 66, 68, 71][78, 80, 84] sts.
Join to work in a round, pm at the join. P around. Then work in St st until sleeve measures [11, 11, 11][11, 11, 12, 12][12, 12.5, 12.5]in/[28, 28, 28][28, 28, 30.5, 30.5][30.5, 32, 32]cm from CO edge. [68, 68, 68][68, 68, 75, 75][75, 78, 78] rnds.

Armhole shaping
On the next rnd work to [3, 3, 3][3, 3, 3, 4][4, 5, 6] sts before m, then BO [6, 6, 6][6, 6, 6, 8][8, 10, 12] sts.
From this point sleeve is worked flat.

Next and all WS rows: P.
Next row (RS): BO [2, 2, 2][2, 3, 3, 3][4, 4, 4] sts in the beg of foll 2 rows.
Dec row (RS): *Ssk, work to last 2 sts, k2tog*.
Repeat dec row on every RS row total of [5, 5, 6][7, 7, 8, 8][10, 10, 10] times.
[38, 39, 39][40, 40, 40, 41][42, 42, 42] sts.
Work straight in patt until armhole measures [4, 4.25, 4.5][4.5, 4.5, 5, 5.25][5.5, 5.75, 6]in/[10, 11, 11.5][11.5, 11.5, 12.5, 13.5][14, 14.5, 15]cm.

Sleeve cap shaping
Row 1 (RS): *Ssk, work to last 2 sts, k2tog*.
Row 2 and all WS rows: P.
Repeat previous 2 rows total of [4, 4, 4][5, 5, 5, 5][5, 5, 5] times.
Next (RS): *Ssk, ssk, work to last 4 sts, k2tog, k2tog*.
WS: P back.
BO [3, 3, 3][3, 3, 3, 3][4, 4, 4] sts in the beg of next 2 rows.
Repeat previous dec row once more.
BO 4 sts in the beg of foll 2 rows.
K [8, 9, 9][8, 8, 8, 9][8, 8, 8]sts.
On next row BO rem [8, 9, 9][8, 8, 8, 9][8, 8, 8]sts.

COLLAR

Using tapestry needle and Main yarn Graft (Kitchener stitch) [19, 19, 20][20, 22, 23, 23][23, 24, 25] shoulder sts together on each side.
Transfer all neckline sts from stitch holders onto circular needle. Rejoin yarn on RS. Continue in established Tab patt and AT THE SAME TIME on first row pick up and k all wraps together with sts they are wrapped around, pick up 1 st on each side at shoulder seams and pick up 1 st per every row worked straight on the neckline.
Work straight in patt for 2in/5cm (or as long as it takes within that proximity to finish last Tab patt).
On last WS row: K all sts.
Next row (RS) BO all sts in p.

FINISHING

Sew sleeves into armholes using Mattress stitch. Soak in luke-warm water, lay flat to dry. Block if needed.
Sew grosgrain ribbon along Tabs edge on both sides (whip stitch). Close the jacket, align bottom parts of clothing snaps and sew them on top of jacket through grosgrain ribbon. Cut 1.5in/4cm pieces of ribbon and sew them onto inside of each Tab. Then sew top parts of clothing snaps through Tab and ribbon.

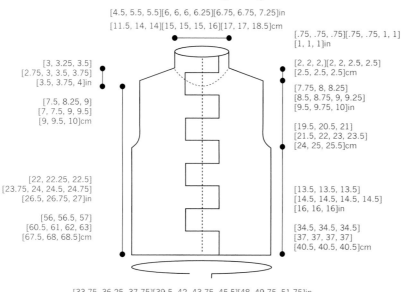

[4, 4, 4.25][4.25, 4.5, 4.75, 4.75][4.75, 5, 5.25]in
[10, 10, 11][11.5, 12, 12, 12][12, 12.5, 13.5]cm

[4.5, 5.5, 5.5][6, 6, 6, 6.25][6.75, 6.75, 7.25]in
[11.5, 14, 14][15, 15, 15, 16][17, 17, 18.5]cm

[.75, .75, .75][.75, .75, 1, 1]
[1, 1, 1]in

[3, 3.25, 3.5]
[2.75, 3, 3.5, 3.75]
[3.5, 3.75, 4]in

[2, 2, 2,][2, 2, 2.5, 2.5]
[2.5, 2.5, 2.5]cm

[7.75, 8, 8.25]
[8.5, 8.75, 9, 9.25]
[9.5, 9.75, 10]in

[7.5, 8.25, 9]
[7, 7.5, 9, 9.5]
[9, 9.5, 10]cm

[19.5, 20.5, 21]
[21.5, 22, 23, 23.5]
[24, 25, 25.5]cm

[22, 22.25, 22.5]
[23.75, 24, 24.5, 24.75]
[26.5, 26.75, 27]in

[13.5, 13.5, 13.5]
[14.5, 14.5, 14.5, 14.5]
[16, 16, 16]in

[56, 56.5, 57]
[60.5, 61, 62, 63]
[67.5, 68, 68.5]cm

[34.5, 34.5, 34.5]
[37, 37, 37, 37]
[40.5, 40.5, 40.5]cm

[33.75, 36.25, 37.75][39.5, 42, 43.75, 45.5][48, 49.75, 51.75]in
[86, 92, 96][100.5, 106.5, 111, 115.5][122, 126.5, 131.5]cm

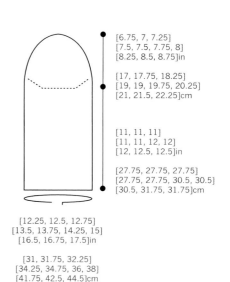

[6.75, 7, 7.25]
[7.5, 7.5, 7.75, 8]
[8.25, 8.5, 8.75]in

[17, 17.75, 18.25]
[19, 19, 19.75, 20.25]
[21, 21.5, 22.25]cm

[11, 11, 11]
[11, 11, 12, 12]
[12, 12.5, 12.5]in

[27.75, 27.75, 27.75]
[27.75, 27.75, 30.5, 30.5]
[30.5, 31.75, 31.75]cm

[12.25, 12.5, 12.75]
[13.5, 13.75, 14.25, 15]
[16.5, 16.75, 17.5]in

[31, 31.75, 32.25]
[34.25, 34.75, 36, 38]
[41.75, 42.5, 44.5]cm

ABBREVIATIONS

alt	alternate
beg	begin(ning)
BO	bind off (cast off)
CC	contrasting color
CN	cable needle
CO	cast on
cont	continue(ing)
dec	decrease(ing)
dpn(s)	double pointed needle(s)
foll	follow(s)(ing)
g	grams
inc	increase(ing)
k	knit
k tbl	knit through back of loop
k2tog	knit 2 sts together (right-leaning decrease)
k2tog tbl	knit 2 sts together through the back loops (left-leaning decrease)
k3tog	knit 3 sts together
kfb	knit into front and back of stitch (increase)
kwise	knitwise, as if to knit
m(s)	marker(s)
m	meter(s)
m1	make 1 stitch (increase between stitches)
m1l	make 1 left
m1r	make 1 right
MC	main color
mm	millimeters
oz	ounce(s)
p	purl

p2tog	purl 2 sts together
p3tog	purl 3 sts together
patt(s)	pattern(s)
pm	place marker
psso	pass slipped stitch over
pwise	purlwise, as if to purl
rem	remaining
rep	repeat
rev St st	reverse stockinette stitch
rib	ribbing
rnd(s)	rounds(s)
RS	right side(s)
sc	single crochet
sl	slip (slip sts purlwise, unless directed otherwise)
sl st	slip stitch
sm	slip marker
ssk	slip 2 sts as if to knit, one at a time, then k those 2 sts together (left-leaning decrease)
st(s)	stitches
St st	stockinette stitch
tbl	though back of loop(s)
tog	together
w&t	wrap and turn
WS	wrong side(s)
wyib	with yarn in back
wyif	with yarn in front
yd(s)	yard(s)
YO	yarn over
**	repeat directions between *s as indicated

NEEDLE CONVERSION

Metric (mm)	US	UK/Canada
2.0	0	14
2.25	1	13
2.75	2	12
3.0	.	11
3.25	3	10
3.5	4	.
3.75	5	9
4.0	6	8
4.5	7	7
5.0	8	6
5.5	9	5
6.0	10	4
6.5	10.5	3
7.0	10.75	2
7.5	.	1
8.0	11	0
9.0	13	00
10.0	15	000

SPECIAL TECHNIQUES

Cast on methods
  Backward loop cast on
  Cabled cast on
  Invisible/Provisional (using crochet hook and scrap yarn) cast on
  Lace cast on (circular in a loop)

Double knitting

Grafting (Kitchener stitch)

I-cord
  Applied I-cord
  I-cord bind off
  Incorporated I-cord

Mattress stitch

Reading charts

Short row shaping

Three-needle bind off

RESOURCES

Yarn
Habu Textiles, LLC
135 West 29th Street
Suite 804
New York, NY 10001

www.habutextiles.com
(212)239-3546

Notions
G Street Fabrics
6250 Seven Corners Center
Falls Church, VA 22044

www.gstreetfabrics.com
(703)241-1700

ACKNOWLEDGMENTS

We want to give thanks to our loved ones, who coped with us through this year long process, while our creativity was being put to life. To our contributing designer, Kirsten Johnstone, for bringing her talent to the table and always being there for us halfway across the globe for any advice, putting sanity to our ramblings, as well as lending amazing wardrobe pieces that have complimented our photoshoot. To our tech editors Alexandra Virgiel and Jenn Jarvis, who emerged alive after being subjected to our unique designing features. Thanks to Takako Ueki, owner of Habu Textiles for donating the materials and being a great visionary who has introduced many of us to these amazing fibers by exposing them to the world outside Japan. This book wouldn't have been possible without the support from our friends Priscilla Meredith and Mac Liaw, who encouraged us from the book's initial stages and helped us in developing our website. Special thanks to Pamela Northrup who, despite immense pressure, managed to finish a garment on small needles in record time. And to Marla Levine and Elspeth Kursh, for their assistance in providing crucial wardrobe additions. To Reiko Kuwamura, for helping us with the Japanese names of our garments. And many thanks to an amazing world of Knitters who kept and continue supporting and believing in our efforts of producing a book of our own. Every day they continue to surprise with their kindness, love and generosity. We are grateful to be able to bring you Ori Ami Knits, where your process of creating garments is enhanced with the visual pleasure of fine photography.
We are thankful to each other for challenging and pushing each other to grow with each experience we have gained throughout the making of this book.